Modern Ideas

IN THE

CHESS OPENINGS

BY

I. A. Horowitz

With 205 diagrams

CORNERSTONE LIBRARY

NEW YORK

Cornerstone Library publications are distributed by
AFFILIATED PUBLISHERS, INC.
Rockefeller Center, 630 Fifth Avenue, New York 20, N. Y.

Manufactured in the United States of America

FOR EDNA

Contents

Foreword

SINCE the publication of the first volume in this series, *How to Win in the Chess Openings*, I have had so many favorable comments from pleased readers that I was encouraged to prepare a second volume along similar lines.

In *How to Win in the Chess Openings* I dealt with variations in the *Giuoco Piano*, Ruy Lopez, French Defense, Sicilian Defense, Queen's Gambit Declined, Réti Opening, English Opening, Alekhine's Defense, and Center Counter Defense. In the present volume I treat eleven different openings, repeating none of the earlier ones. The two books may therefore be read independently of each other, though the method is the same in both.

The general idea of each opening is first explained; then individual moves are analyzed on a move-to-move basis and also in terms of their relation to the plan of the opening as a whole. To many readers it comes as a revelation that there *is* a general plan for each opening, and that knowing this plan is a great help in playing better chess.

But to have a plan is not enough—you have to see how the plan works out in practical play. Each opening discussion is therefore followed by a "Chess Movie"—an actual game profusely illustrated in diagrams. In these games you can see how a player benefits by following the plan of the opening, how another comes to grief by disregarding the plan.

A new feature is the group of twenty-two illustrative games in the last chapter, illustrating vital details of theory in the openings studied in this book. In many cases these games are continuations of the main line of analysis in each of the preceding chapters. By playing over these games, the reader can arrive at a more precise judgment of the model variations. As I wrote in the previous volume, "It is clear that with understanding will come many victories."

I. A. HOROWITZ

MODERN IDEAS IN THE
CHESS OPENINGS

1

A Review of the Principles of Opening Play

IN THE good old days, map makers used to fill in the space devoted to Central Africa with the legend: "Here be monsters." This is the feeling that most chessplayers have when they consult an opening manual with a thousand tabular columns of opening play, with innumerable side lines, variations, and references to thousands of master games.

Aside from the forbidding look of such compilations, they omit what the student needs above all: a survey of the *principles* of good opening play. Not knowing what to look for, he is only confused and exasperated by the richness of the material. Hence, before we proceed to study individual openings, we shall want to familiarize ourselves with some of the grand principles that rule all opening play.*

* These principles are explained in great detail, with many examples, in *How to Win in the Chess Openings*.

The opening stage is usually limited to the first twelve or so moves. It is that part of the game in which we develop our forces, or prepare to develop them. We do not aim for ultimate goals at the very start—we do not try for checkmate right off the reel.

Generally, it is small advantages that we seek at the start. We try to avoid Pawn weaknesses; we try to avoid loss of material. We strive to control the important center squares—particularly K4 and Q4 in each camp. We try to develop our pieces so that they are placed in the center or bearing down on the center. If they are so placed, they can reach any part of the board rapidly and with great effect.

To win material is important at any time—in the opening as well as later on. Why? Because a Pawn has the ability to become a Queen if it reaches the eighth rank unharmed, giving its possessor a decisive material advantage.

If we can win greater material than a Pawn, so much the better. That is why it is important to know the relative value of the forces.

Thus, a Knight is worth about three Pawns. The Bishop has a *slightly* greater value in most cases. The Rook is worth five Pawns—more than a Bishop or Knight. The Queen, the strongest of the forces, is worth nine Pawns. That is to say, more than a Rook and Bishop or Rook and Knight, but somewhat less than two Rooks.

It is vital to be familiar with these relative values, for there are innumerable cases of possible exchange or capture where we have to be guided by the relative values of the pieces involved. This is our main guide in answering the questions: Do I capture? Do I exchange? Do I let him capture? Do I let him exchange? Do I retreat? Do I force him to retreat?

Though these problems often arise in the opening stage, you are not likely to win large material in the opening unless your opponent blunders crassly. Also, you must remember that these values are modified by extraordinary circumstances. A Pawn that administers checkmate is worth a million dollars!

An undeveloped Knight or a Queen far off from the scene of action may be worth far less than its academic value. So, it is not only relative value that matters; you must realize that particular forces that are especially active are thereby more valuable, while inactive forces depreciate in value.

Development, we know, is important in the opening. Generally you want to bring out your Knights first, because their best squares are easy to hit on. The King Knight goes almost invariably to KB3, from where it hits at the important center squares Q4 or K5. (Playing this piece to KR3 will deprive it of practically all influence on the center.)

The Bishops generally come out after the Knights, as it is not always clear at the very beginning which square is best for a Bishop.

The development of the Queen can be deferred still more, because she is only likely to be harried by hostile pieces of lesser value. As a rule, the Queen will be developed only when the battle lines are already drawn. Sometimes the Queen will be played to K2 or Q2 or QB2 to make room for a Rook move to a center square. But this is unlikely to happen before the eighth move or thereabouts. The Rooks take quite a while to be brought into play—generally after castling. It takes time until the pieces are developed (moved from their original squares on the back row). Until the pieces are played out, the Rooks are unable to move along the back row.

To what squares should the Rooks be played? That will be determined by the existence of open files. As we know, open files are created by Pawn captures or recaptures, so that gives us the key to placing the Rooks. To post a Rook on a file that is closed and is likely to be closed means that we are not getting the full value of the Rook's power and possibilities. Like the other pieces, the Rook belongs on lines where it has mobility.

Castling (the combined move of Rook and King) is almost always a valuable contribution to development. The Rook is brought nearer to the center, and at the same time the King is removed from the center so that its presence will not hamper the action of the other pieces. (Castling is also a help by making the King safer. This eases the defensive burden imposed on our forces.)

Try to be economical in developing. Inexperienced players often make the mistake of moving one piece several times without appreciably increasing its effectiveness—and at the same time they neglect their other pieces.

One of the great problems of economical developing is deciding whether a Pawn capture in the opening costs too much time. It takes practice and experience to be able to appraise such situations accurately. Be guided, also, by your own temperament. If you chafe under the need for being on the defensive, avoid spending time on Pawn-grabbing if it means yielding the initiative to your opponent.

Be wary of weakening your Pawns; try to weaken your opponent's Pawns. What does this mean in concrete language?

There are various kinds of weak Pawns. An isolated Pawn, for example, is one which has no Pawns of its own color on neighboring files, and therefore cannot be protected by Pawns. It has to be protected by pieces. Obviously it is good policy to train your guns on your opponent's isolated Pawn, if he has one.

A doubled Pawn is also a weakness to some extent, because two Pawns on the same file cannot give each other protection. A doubled, isolated Pawn is an even worse weakness. Of course, doubled Pawns offer a certain amount of compensation: their very existence guarantees an open file—sometimes two open files—on which your Rooks can be active.

One of the most flagrant weaknesses in Pawn structure comes about when a Pawn has been advanced into enemy territory. Such overextended Pawns make easy targets and at the same time cost their defender much time and effort to keep them safeguarded.

Pawn "holes" are another type of weakness frequently encountered. A "hole" is a square that cannot be guarded by

Pawns because the Pawns on the neighboring files have already advanced. Thus, on page 129, Black's K4 square is a hole because his King Bishop Pawn and Queen Pawn can no longer protect that square (both ... P-KB3 and ... P-Q3 are impossible).

To complete the roster of Pawn weaknesses, we must mention the backward Pawn. This type of Pawn has neighbors, but they have already advanced and are thus unable to guard the backward Pawn. On page 129, Black's King Pawn is a backward Pawn.

But Pawns are not always weaknesses. Sometimes they can be remarkably powerful. The center Pawn, for example, which controls a vital square by depriving hostile pieces of access to that square, is playing a role of the greatest value.

Even more valuable are passed Pawns—those whose advance is not impeded by hostile Pawns on neighboring files. A passed Pawn is a potential Queen, and has already surmounted one of the greatest obstacles to queening.

It is this factor that gives Pawn majorities their great importance. If you have three Pawns to your opponent's two on the Queen-side, you are said to have the Queen-side majority of Pawns. By judicious advance and exchange, your three-to-two majority should eventually result in a passed Pawn. You should therefore view a Pawn majority as a potential passed Pawn.

Finally, Pawns are of enormous value in opening lines by capture or recapture. This is a point that cannot be stressed too highly. If you keep your eye on Pawn play in games that you study, you will observe again and again that the opening of lines is made possible in most cases by well-timed Pawn moves. In master play a Pawn—occasionally more than one Pawn—is sacrificed to open up a line for a decisive attack. We admire the incisive play that winds up the game, but if anything, we ought to admire even more the elegant Pawn move that makes it all possible.

From this point it is logical to proceed to the idea that the

Pawn position gives us a great many priceless pointers on how to plan. The pattern of the Pawns after the tenth move or so usually tells us how Bishops are placed most effectively, where the Knights should head, what the Rooks can accomplish, what targets to aim for, what lines to open.

If this notion strikes you as a novel one, turn to the following chapters, and see how the nature of the Pawn position influences the plan of the game. In one opening after another, you will observe that the Pawn position sets the "tone" of the remaining play.

For example: in the Center Game, White's Pawn move 2 P-Q4 opens up the game too soon. In the Danish, the Pawn sacrifices set off a heated controversy of development versus material. In the King's Gambit, the opening struggle centers about White's attempt to pre-empt the center with the Pawn thrust 2 P-KB4. In Philidor's Defense, Black remains with a permanently constricted position after the Pawn move 2 ... P-Q3.

And so it goes. Test this idea on the openings treated in this book, and on all openings in general. The Pawn pattern will teach you a great deal and sharpen your eye for the possibilities inherent in any given position.

2

The typical position in the Center Game

Center Game

Perfect symmetry and nearly perfect balance mark the original position of the chess game. With the exception of the first move, which is endowed to White and from which springs a minimal initiative, all is equal. From that first move, however, unlike and variable factors—time, space, and force—come into play. And immediately the equilibrium is upset.

When a Pawn is paired off against an opposing Pawn, or a Knight for a Knight, etc., it is easy to see that, as far as material goes, an even relationship exists. When an open line, however, is measured against a tempo or a strategic square against some other complement—that is, intangibles against intangibles—real skill is required for appraising the net plus or minus.

So it is with the Center Game proper. After the moves *1* P-K4, P-K4; White plays *2* P-Q4 in order to open lines quickly—the Queen file and the diagonal for the Queen Bishop. Moreover, he collapses Black's strong point, his K4, in one fell move. On the face of it, consequently, the move is good; but there is one drawback. In recapturing the Pawn, *White brings his Queen out early*. The White Queen is vulnerable, and thus Black is able to gain one move. One tiny tempo, and that is all that is necessary to weight the scale in favor of the defender. So delicately are the scales balanced.

Favorable opinion is on the side of the defender. In modern times the opening has been championed by such masters as Mieses, Spielmann, and Tartakover, but without success.

The Center Game dates from Polerio, 1590, although White's third move *3* QxP was first noticed in Stamma, 1737.

The Center Game arises as follows:

1	P-K4	P-K4
2	P-Q4	. . . .

The Center Game. The advance of the Queen Pawn serves three purposes: (1) it opens the Queen file for White; (2) it releases White's Queen Bishop for immediate action; (3) it suggests an exchange of center Pawns, after which White's King Pawn will remain in a dominating position, striking the enemy squares Q5 and KB5, while its counterpart, Black's Queen Pawn, will be backward, touching squares only within its own half of the board.

To capture is best. The alternatives leave much to be desired. For instance, if Black defends with *2* ... P-Q3, then *3* PxP, PxP; *4* QxQch, KxQ; and Black has forfeited the privilege of castling. If *2* ... N-QB3; *3* PxP, NxP; *4* P-KB4, White usurps the center. This line, incidentally, has the earmarks of hypermodernism insofar as Black's Knight provokes the advance of White's Pawns with a view to leaving them weak and as fixed targets.

2 .... **PxP**

The counterattack by 2 ... N-KB3 leaves White with the superior game after 3 PxP, NxP 4 Q-Q5, N-B4, 5 B-B4. Then 5 ... N-K3 grants White a more flourishing development while 5 ... Q-K2 causes obstruction in Black's ranks.

3 **QxP** ....

The Center Game proper. Other moves, such as 3 N-KB3 or 3 B-QB4, although branches of the Center Game, are openings in their own right.

3 .... **N-QB3**

Developing with gain of tempo by attacking the Queen. This one move is Black's compensation for the advantages that have accrued to White thus far.

The recommended book line. The strategic idea involved here is for White to swing his Queen eventually to KN3 (toward where he hopes the Black Monarch will be), castle Queen-side, and exert pressure on the open Queen file.

Black's problem is to find suitable counterplay with a plan of his own.

Alternatives for White are 4 Q-B4, 4 Q-R4, and 4 Q-Q1.

4 Q-B4 gives Black a free and easy game after the moves 4 ... N-B3; 5 N-QB3, P-Q4! This tricky, temporary sacrifice of a Pawn solves all of Black's problems of development. For example, after 5 PxP, N-QN5 (simultaneously attacking the Queen Pawn and the Queen Bishop Pawn); Black must recover the Pawn. Or, in this line, if 5 NxP, NxN; 6 PxN, N-N5; again Black must recover the Pawn.

4 Q-K3   . . . .

4 Q-R4 is the most desirable of the alternatives, although, up to the present, White has not been able to demonstrate any advantage from it. A line of play might follow this order: 4 Q-R4, B-B4; 5 N-KB3, P-Q3; 6 N-B3, KN-K2; 7 B-KN5, B-Q2. Black appears to have sufficient resources, mainly because of the threat of discovering an attack on White's Queen.

This writer holds a deep conviction that somewhere along the line, White might improve his technique, although he is not prepared at the moment to present any satisfactory suggestion.

4 Q-Q1 fails inasmuch as the tempo presented to Black counterbalances the advantages gained by White's second move.

4 . . . .   N-B3!

This star move dates back to an analysis by Berger in 1884. Any other move permits White to further his grand plan without much opposition.

The move invites tricky play.

5 **N-QB3** ....

5 P-K5 puts Black to the test. It can be refuted, however, with correct play, thus: 5 P-K5, N-KN5; 6 Q-K2, P-Q3; 7 P-KB3, N-R3; 8 PxPch, B-K3; 9 BxN, Q-R5ch; with an attack worth the Pawn.

In this line, Black can sacrifice a piece on his seventh move with 7 ... KNxKP, but White should come out on top. The play might go as follows: 7 ... KNxKP; 8 P-KB4, N-Q5; 9 Q-K4, P-QB4; 10 N-QR3, B-B4; 11 Q-K3, Q-R4ch; 12 K-B2!, O-O-O; 13 PxN, PxP; 14 P-B3, N-B3; 15 N-B4.

5 .... **B-K2**

Good also is 5 ... B-N5; 6 B-Q2, O-O; 7 O-O-O, R-K1; 8 Q-N3, NxP!; 9 NxN, RxN; 10 B-KB4, Q-B3!; 11 N-R3, P-Q3; 12 B-Q3, N-Q5!; 13 B-K3, R-N5; 14 BxN, RxB; 15 P-QB3, BxP; 16 PxB; R-KN5; 17 Q-K3, QxQBPch; 18 B-B2, QxQch; 19 PxQ, RxP.

It is to be observed that the onus of precision play, however, rests with Black in this variation. One misstep could be fatal.

6 **B-Q2** ....

Developing apace and making ready for Queen-side castling, which is part of the grand strategic plan.

6 . . . .   **P-Q4!**

The correct procedure. If Black submits to ... P-Q3 out of choice or circumstance, White's plan will shape up effectively; whereas after his last move, Black should experience no development problems.

7 PxP   NxP
8 NxN   QxN

Observe that Black enjoys the lead in development, traceable to White's early Queen moves.

9 N-K2   . . . .

White still eyes the prospects of castling Queen-side and intends to fortify his Queen Rook Pawn and drive Black's Queen by continuing with N-B3.

9 . . . .   **B-KN5**

But this move restrains the execution of White's plan. Now, if *10* N-B3, White will be unable to castle as his King cannot pass the line of Black's Queen Bishop.

>   *10* **N-B4**   ....

White accommodates himself to the change.

>   *10* **Q-Q2**
>   *11* **P-KB3**   ....

White drives the Bishop so as to make Queen-side castling possible.

>   *11* ....   **O-O-O!**

Oddly enough, it is Black who castles first on the long side. The move, however, offers a piece. Just as good is *11* ... B-KB4, although the text sets a trap.

>   *12* **O-O-O**   ....

Capturing the piece will get White into trouble, thus: *12* PxB, B-R5ch; *13* K-Q1 (*13* P-KN3 loses), KR-K1; *14* Q-Q3, QxPch; *15* B-K2, RxB; *16* QxR, QxN; *17* K-B1, N-Q5; with a powerful attack.

>   *12* **B-KB4**
>   *13* **B-Q3**   ....

Since White's plan has gone awry, he is content to draw and offers a friendly exchange of material.

13 ....   **B-B3**

But it is Black who enjoys the initiative and plays for whatever the position offers.

14 **BxB**   **QxB**
15 **KR-K1**   **N-Q5**

Black has the better game.

Conclusions and recommendations

While the Center Game proper theoretically places no great obstacles in the way of the defender, it does burden him with the necessity of finding innumerably difficult and treacherous moves.

The line beginning with *1* P-K4, P-K4; *2* P-Q4, PxP; *3* QxP, N-QB3; *4* Q-R4 has met with tournament reverses, up to the present. Sometime, somewhere, this line will be bolstered, and White will enjoy the benefit of a new opening weapon.

Chess Movie

O-O-O OH! OH!

THE EVOLUTION of an opening depicts any number of plausible ideas, which have come and gone, and left their imprint in the golden treasury of chess. Here Russian grandmaster Tchigorin (White) refutes Mackenzie's rational defense to the Center Game. The scene is Vienna, 1882. The game begins with the moves: *1* P-K4, P-K4; *2* P-Q4, PxP; *3* QxP, N-QB3; *4* Q-K3. (Continue from Diagram 1.)

1 Mackenzie adopts an old-fashioned defense. 4 ... P-KN3 is the move. Tchigorin continues with the grand plan. There follows 5 B-Q2, B-N2; 6 N-QB3, P-Q3. White is to castle long and attack on the other wing, where he hopes the opposing monarch will be. Black develops systematically.

2 7 P-B4 signals White's plan, and Black continues his development apace with 7 ... KN-K2. There follows 8 O-O-O, B-K3; 9 N-B3, Q-Q2. Black is developing and jockeying at the same time. He has not determined to castle on the King-side; the Queen-side may do too.

17

3 *10* N-Q5 is White's move, and Black follows with *10* ... O-O-O. And why not? Is White not ready for him on the other wing? There follows *11* B-B3, BxB; *12* QxB, N-QN1. Just in time, Black manages to avoid the menacing checkmate to his Queen! Still Black suffers from a backward game.

4 White accommodates himself to the new conditions. Black's King is on the Queen-side, and he heads for that direction. *13* Q-R3 is the move. Black plays *13* ... BxN, and *14* PxB, Q-B4 follows. Two Pawns are attacked. White defends one with *15* P-KN3, and Black takes one with *15* ... NxP.

5 White inches in with *16* N-Q4, and Black retires with *16* ... Q-Q2. White comes closer with *17* N-N5, and Black defends with *17* ... P-QB3. Then follows *18* NxRPch, and the Black monarch is budged from his haven with *18* ... K-B2. Material is even, but White is gaining ground.

6 The time has come for a quickening pace. *19* RxN! shatters Black's defensive barrier. Black replies *19* ... PxR; and there follows *20* B-N5 driving the enemy Queen. Black plays *20* ... Q-K3 and then comes *21* Q-B3ch, K-N3. White draws a long bead on the Black King. The end is in sight.

7 But first the Black Queen must be removed from the vital scene. 22 R-K1 is the move. Black takes two Rooks for the Queen by playing 22 ... KxN. There follows 23 RxQ, PxR. Then White aims at the King with 24 Q-K3ch, and Black retreats with 24 ... K-R1. The King is cornered.

8 Now comes the fatal incursion. The sequel is 25 Q-R3ch, N-R3; 26 BxN, PxB; 27 QxPch, K-N1. The monarch is at White's mercy. A perpetual check is the least of his troubles. Is that, however, enough compensation for White's valor? The answer is written on the next panel.

9 28 Q-N6ch puts the opposing monarch in position. 28 ... K-B1 is the move. Then 29 P-QN4 is the follow-up. A Queen and two passed Pawns against a lone King ought to be more than sufficient to decide the fate of the game, if no reinforcements are available. Is there any defense?

10 Quickly, Black plays 29 ... KR-K1. He feints a threat with his King Pawn and builds a psychological defense. White plays 30 Q-R7, and Black advances 30 ... P-K4. White follows with 31 P-N5, and there is no defense to the further advance of this mighty Pawn. Black resigns.

3

A typical position in the Danish

Danish Gambit

ONCE UPON A time it was considered ungentlemanly to decline a gambit. Then it was that the King's Gambit, the Max Lange, the Evans, and the Danish, among others, saw their heyday.

In those blissfully romantic days, chess technique was not fully developed. Not yet mastered was the art of sound defense. Advantages in time and space—the goal of the gambit—were given top rating. Material was looked upon askance. During this profligate era, the Danish was born. For the true

Danish, extended to its thematic finale, involves the sacrifice of two Pawns, in return for rapid development.

This enterprising opening, according to historian H. J. R. Murray, was played by a Danish jurist in Jutland in the 1830's. It was well known in Scandinavian countries before Von der Lasa, the Prussian Ambassador at Copenhagen, introduced it generally in 1867. And it was first noted in the game Lindehn versus Swanberg, 1859.

Today it is considered foolhardy to decline a real gambit. "Take first and look later" is the guiding principle. For accent is on material! Hard-boiled cynicism has brought about the pragmatic transition. For the gambiteer, self-handicapped and under constant pressure to convert intangible assets into something real, often fails of his mark. Lack of force and even lack of *sitzfleisch* undo him.

Despite these qualms, gambiteers will not be suppressed. Control of the center and two powerful Bishops, exercising full sway on commanding diagonals are inducements for the Danish, in particular. And, in general for gambits in over-the-board play, there is an actual, though intangible, advantage in pressuring a queasy opponent.

The Danish arises as follows:

1	P-K4	P-K4
2	P-Q4	PxP
3	P-QB3	. . . .

3 QxP is the Center Game proper. (See the previous chapter.)

The text move is the first step in the Danish Gambit. It is the offer of a Pawn in return for development.

3 ....   **PxP**

This is in line with the guiding principle: "Take first and look later." As a matter of fact, however, no other Black move is apt to produce an advantage. Black, moreover, must do something about White's threat to play 4 PxP and regain his Pawn and remain with a powerful Pawn center.

An alternative for Black is 3 ... P-Q4; after which the game also becomes lively. Then 4 KPxP, QxP; 5 PxP, N-QB3; 6 N-KB3, B-N5; 7 B-K2, N-B3; 8 N-B3, Q-QR4; White's minimal lead in development overshadows the disadvantage of his isolated Pawn.

4 B-QB4   ....

This move aims primarily at the most vulnerable square in Black's camp—Black's KB2. One of White's ideas is to concentrate enough pressure on that square, during the future course of the game, so as to make it embarrassing for the defender.

In this position, however, Alekhine warmly recommends 4 NxP. The line might run as follows: 4 ... P-Q3; 5 B-QB4, N-QB3; 6 N-B3, B-K3!; 7 B-Q5, N-B3; 8 O-O, B-K2; with a good game for Black. For example, if 9 BxB, PxB; 10 Q-N3, Q-B1; and Black stands well. The spirit of the gambit, moreover, dictates the text move—the sacrifice of a second Pawn—whose object is the gain of time and space in return for material.

Black need not go all out in accepting the gambit. He can pull in his horns with 4 ... P-Q3 and lead to the variation given in the preceding note. Or he might continue with 4 ... N-QB3; 5 N-B3, B-B4; 6 NxP, P-Q3; 7 Q-N3, Q-Q2; 8 N-Q5, KN-K2; 9 Q-B3, O-O; 10 O-O, NxN; 11 PxN, N-K4; 12 NxN, PxN; 13 QxP, B-Q3; with about equal chances.

4 ....   **PxP**

The text move gives Black a plus of two Pawns for the inferior position. It is, however, the only clear-cut way of refuting the gambit.

5 **BxP**   ....
(See Photo)

The Danish proper. Observe the commanding sweep of both of White's Bishops. Observe also that White maintains control of the center—but that he is two Pawns behind.

The question is: Can White exploit his advantages before Black is able to consolidate?

5 ....   **P-QB3**

The first move of a deep defensive plan. The move is sharp and flexible. The Pawn at QB3 serves as a barrier, eliminates a White threat of entering at White's Q5, and also serves as a prop for a later move of ... P-Q4 or ... P-QN4.

The recommended book line at this point runs as follows: 5 ... P-Q4; 6 KBxP, N-KB3; 7 BxPch, KxB; 8 QxQ, B-N5ch, 9 Q-Q2, BxQch; 10 NxB, P-B4.

At one time, authorities agreed that Black enjoyed the better chances on account of his Queen-side Pawn majority, which can be mobilized rapidly. It was thought that White's King-side majority could be checked with the assistance of the Black King. The books concur in this belief. A number of unofficial games, however, challenges this conclusion. For, after 11 N-KB3, Black's King is somewhat of a target, and, instead of hindering the adverse Pawns, actually promotes their advance.

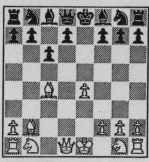

6 **N-QB3**   . . . .

A good developing move, although White has the option of a number of good developing moves at this stage. In each case, however, Black resorts to the same kind of defense that he sets up here and manages to come out on top.

Some of White's possibilities are crafty and must be handled with care. For instance, if 6 P-K5, Black must batter down White's restraining hold on the Black Pawns. This is done in the following manner: 6 ... Q-K2, threatening ... P-Q4 as well as ... Q-N5ch, each of which routs the White men. White then has no better than 7 K-B1. Then, if Black persists with 7 ... P-Q4; 8 PxP e.p., QxP; 9 QxQ, BxQ; 10 BxNP wins the Rook. Therefore, if 6 P-K5, Q-K2; 7 K-B1, P-B3. Now, whatever White does, Black must enforce ... P-Q4 and consolidate his forces and obtain a free and easy development.

Incidentally, if 6 Q-N3, Q-K2; Black's threat of ... P-Q4 as well as ... Q-N5ch bogs down White's assault.

It should be borne in mind that Black is two Pawns ahead. If necessary, he is willing to part with one of them (or even both) in order to emerge with the better position.

6 . . . .   **P-Q3**

This move is played not merely to free Black's Queen Bishop. It is part and parcel of a system of defense. The Pawn at Q3 is part of the barrier to enemy incursion.

Black's over-all plan is to prevent any breach in his Pawn position and then slowly bring out his forces and remain with material plus.

7 N-B3 . . . .

There is no crushing or even impetuous rejoinder. Consequently, White must develop apace. His hope is that after all his men are brought out, he will be able to find or provoke a weakness in Black's camp.

7 . . . . N-Q2

This is the third step in the defensive plan. Watch the maneuver of the Queen Knight to its final destination.

8 O-O . . . .

Again, development goes on steadily. If 8 Q-N3, Black defends with ... Q-K2 and later drives the Queen with ... N-B4.

8 . . . . N-B4

Black is for choice. There are a number of good continuations at his disposal. He can play ... B-K3 and compel the retreat or exchange of White's mighty King Bishop. Then he can continue with his King-side development, until it is complete. In the interim, White has no penetrating moves or such as will increase the pressure before Black is able to develop and consolidate. In the long run, the extra two Pawns will make themselves felt.

Conclusions and recommendations

Like most gambits, the Danish leads to exciting play. The attacker always enjoys the game, at least during the early stages. Against accurate defense, however, the attack peters out, and then the defender reaps his material reward.

Unless some way can be found to breach the barrier set up by Black, beginning with his third move, the Danish will be relegated to use by the dilettante, who cares little about book plays or exactitude.

At present, it appears that the Danish proper is refuted.

Chess Movie

THE DANISH DOES IT

WHEN IS A Pawn not a Pawn? When it is dished up in a Danish, of course. Then it is only a decoy to lure enemy men away from their King. Janowski and Soldatenkoff (White) offer two Pawns to ambush the mighty Lasker and Taubenhaus in this brilliant miniature, played at Paris, 1909. It opens with *1* P-K4, P-K4; *2* P-Q4, PxP; *3* P-QB3, PxP; *4* B-QB4, PxP; *5* BxP, reaching the position in Diagram 1.

1 The Black team treats the position the same as any other. Development is accented: 5 ... N-KB3 is the move. This provokes the reply, *6* P-K5, driving the Knight from its post. Then follows *6* ... B-N5ch. Black's plan is to cut down material or compel White's King to move.

2 White interposes *7* N-B3, and Black pins the adverse King Pawn with *7* ... Q-K2. White breaks the pin with *8* N-K2, and Black enters *8* ... N-K5. Both sides are happy—White, because his development is supreme—Black, because he is managing to swap forces. What now?

3 More men to battle is White's plan as he plays 9 O-O. Less men is Black's idea as he swaps: *9 ... NxN; 10 BxN, BxB.* White recaptures *11 NxB,* and off to safety goes the Black monarch with *11 ... O-O.* (Safety is only relative. The King must yet rebuff a few enemy forces.)

4 White penetrates with *12 N-Q5!* offering, as it were, even another Pawn. And Black captures *12 ... QxP.* He'll be hanged for a sheep rather than a lamb. With three Pawns to the good, Black's prospects are promising. It is White's turn, however, and the game is young.

5 First comes *13 R-K1,* gaining another valuable tempo. Black retreats *13 ... Q-Q3.* Then follows *14 Q-R5,* fixing the sights on the enemy King. Already the threats are mounting, and there is little to be done about them. Black's entire Queen's wing is bottled up, pathetically.

6 Black is sadly lacking the time, which he so readily gave up in the beginning. He continues with *14 ... P-QB3,* attacking White's critter. White replies startlingly with *15 N-B7!* He must clear the path of the King Bishop. Material gain is only a secondary consideration.

7 The Knight is immune. (If *14 ... QxN;* Black is checkmated in two!) Black tries to make the most of a bad position and continues with *15 ... P-KN3.* White replies *16 Q-R6,* and now a piece goes with *16 ... QxN.* White can hardly give up more material. He needs a mating force.

8 Yet White does give up more. *17 BxPch!* is the move. Black has no choice; he plays *17 ... KxB.* Then follows *18 QxRPch!,* and the Black King advances, *18 ... K-B3.* The monarch is due for a walk—one of those compulsory walks, with a bayonet at his midriff. All is gloom in the Black camp.

9 *19 Q-R4ch* forces the retreat *19 ... K-N2.* Then follows *20 R-K7ch.* Black interposes *20 ... R-B2.* For a moment, it appears that Black is squirming out. But ho! *21 Q-Q4ch* places the King in target range. The King retreats *21 ... K-B1.* He is to be forced into the open for the last time.

10 A combination winds up the game in magnificent style. *22 Q-R8ch!* is the first move. Black plays *22 ... KxR.* Now follows *23 R-K1ch.* Black plays *22 ... K-Q3. 24 Q-K5ch* is checkmate. All the King's horses and all the King's men are quite unable to save the King.

4

The typical position in the King's Gambit

King's Gambit

Long before basic principles of chess were expressed in so many words, competent players essayed correct stratagems. The importance of controlling the center while promoting development—the paramount tenet for openings today—for example, was recognized as far back as 1561, when Lopez inaugurated the King's Gambit.

After the moves, *1 P-K4, P-K4*; White offers a Pawn with *2 P-KB4*. This simple move embodies a dual purpose, which strikes at the heart of opening theory. It aims to decoy the staunch enemy King Pawn from its occupation of the center proper and, at the same time, it opens the King Bishop file for future use. Whether these gains offset the value of a Pawn, however, is the moot question.

In 1842, the King's Gambit was analyzed at length by Jaenisch, who enthusiastically designated it "an imperishable monument of human wisdom," for it had evolved during the course of centuries and was far from obsolete. A while later, it languished under a niggardly fashion for closed games that became prevalent and then made its reappearance at the Gambit Tournaments of Abbazia, 1912, and Baden, 1914. There it was shown that Black could obtain equality by returning the extra Pawn. Sporadic attempts to revive the popularity of the King's Gambit have just about fallen short of their mark. The present trend, however, is toward a revival of the gambit.

The King's Gambit arises as follows:

> 1 P-K4   P-K4
> 2 P-KB4   . . . .

The King's Gambit—so called because White proffers a Pawn on the King's side of the board.

The immediate purpose of the sacrifice is to sidetrack Black's King Pawn from the central zone and enable White to gain a preponderance in that sector. The long-term purpose is to open the King Bishop file for future use. Since the most vulnerable point in Black's camp is his KB2, it is clear that an open line leading directly to that square enhances White's prospects of assault.

Unlike the Queen's Gambit, the offer of the gambit Pawn here is firm; the Pawn cannot be retrieved at will. Under the circumstances, White is prepared to give up material for compensating gain in space and mobility. Whether one offsets the other is the issue.

> 2 . . . .   PxP

As a general principle, it is always best to accept a gambit, with a view to returning the material at an auspicious moment, when the material plus can be converted to gain in other directions. Opinion on the acceptance of the King's Gambit, however, is divided. There are those who prefer the prospects of the gambit declined or the countergambit.

Now Black is a Pawn to the good and it is up to White to capitalize on his advantages—the control of the center, the open King Bishop file, and the usual minimal initiative—by exploiting them to the full.

The King's Gambit Declined—2 ... B-B4—and the Falkbeer Counter Gambit—2 ... P-Q4—will be discussed in the next chapter.

3 **N-KB3**   . . . .

After the text move, the opening is technically known as the King Knight's Gambit as distinguished from 3 B-B4, which is the Bishop's Gambit.

Whereas the latter was in vogue for many years, it is now believed that the former is the sounder of the two and sets up greater problems for the defender.

If 3 B-B4, however, the game might continue as follows: 3 ... N-KB3; 4 N-QB3, P-B3!; 5 Q-B3, P-Q4; 6 PxP, B-Q3; 7 P-Q3, B-KN5; 8 Q-B2, O-O; 9 BxP, R-K1ch; 10 K-B1, P-QN4; 11 B-QN3, P-N5; 12 QN-K2, NxP; with the better game for Black.

It is to be observed in the above line that after 3 ... N-KB3; if White thrusts forward with 4 P-K5, Black parries with 4 ... P-Q4!; and if then 5 PxN, PxB; Black's prospects are superior.

In this connection, it ought to be noted for future reference that this tactical parry (... P-Q4!) applies as well to similar situations in other openings, as well as the King's Gambit.

The text, a good developing move, bears on the center.

3 ....   **B-K2**

At the present moment in the evolution of the defense, the text move supersedes the perennial 3 ... N-KB3 and 3 ... P-Q4. These moves have been temporarily shelved, because of some refinements in White's play, which seem to give the first player the upper hand.

For example, 3 ... N-KB3; 4 P-K5, N-R4; 5 P-Q4, P-Q4; 6 N-B3, P-KN4; 7 B-K2, P-N5; 8 O-O!, R-N1!; 9 N-K1, B-R3; 10 B-Q3, B-K3; 11 N-K2!, Q-R5; 12 BxBP. Black's Pawn structure is inferior and his offensive is spent.

Or 3 ... P-Q4; 4 PxP, N-KB3; 5 B-N5ch, P-B3; 6 PxP, PxP; 7 B-B4, B-Q3; 8 Q-K2ch, Q-K2; 9 QxQch, KxQ; 10 P-Q4, B-KB4; 11 N-K5, BxN; 12 PxB, N-Q4; 13 BxN, with advantage for White.

Of course, any new move or idea could easily rehabilitate either of the above lines. They are, however, still to be discovered.

The traditional defense of the gambit Pawn—3 ... P-KN4—has long since been relegated to limbo. This move might be a prelude to the following course: 3 ... P-KN4; 4 P-KR4!, P-N5; 5 N-K5, N-KB3; 6 P-Q4, P-Q3; 7 N-Q3, NxP; 8 BxP, Q-K2;

9 Q-K2, B-N2; *10* P-B3, P-KR4; *11* N-Q2, NxN; *12* KxN with
superiority for White. The defect in this defense is that White
can exploit Black's weakened King-side Pawn structure and
then make penetrating inroads into the Black King's camp.

Oddly enough, the move that offers Black the best chance,
according to the "book," is the puny *3 . . .* P-KR3, known as
Becker's Defense. This move, however, is so much anathema
to the principles of good chess (at least in the mind of this
scribe), that it can hardly be recommended, even if good! Its
point is that it is preparatory to defending the gambit Pawn
with *. . .* P-KN4. At the same time, it exercises a temporizing
effect, waiting for White's next move. Clearly, White can
hardly afford, after *3 . . .* P-KR3, to continue with *4* P-KR4 to
prevent Black from playing *. . .* P-KN4. For, in that case,
White disrupts his own King-side Pawn formation, without
breaching Black's. Accordingly, White must continue his development, with some such move as *4* B-B4. Then Black can
essay *4 . . .* P-KN4; and the sting is taken out of White's
stroke of *5* P-KR4. This line might run as follows: *3 . . .* P-KR3;
4 B-B4, P-KN4; *5* O-O, B-N2; *6* P-Q4, P-Q3. The position is
approximately even, since Black's Pawn plus is offset by White's
control of the center.

That Black can afford to neglect his development by playing so many Pawn moves in a row, such as *2 . . .* PxP, *3 . . .*
P-KB3, *4 . . .* P-KN4, is questionable. This idea is bound to fall
from grace, just as soon as the masters seriously apply themselves to discover its refutation.

A point in favor of the text move, *3 . . .* B-K2, as against
3 . . . N-KB3, is that White cannot advance his Pawn to K5
and drive the opposing Knight to KR4, where it is more or
less on a limb.

4 B-B4   . . . .

White continues his development apace, controls the center,
and bears down on the vulnerable point in Black's camp, his
KB2 square.

4 ....   N-KB3!

A suggestion credited to Schlechter. *4 ... B-R5ch*, known as the Cunningham Gambit, is too risky. On the face of it, it is doomed. Black can hardly afford to neglect his development, even for the sake of forcing the adverse King to move. This line might run as follows: *4 ... B-R5ch; 5 K-B1, P-Q4; 6 BxP, N-KB3; 7 N-B3, O-O; 8 P-Q4, P-B3; 9 B-N3, B-N5; 10 QBxP, N-R4; 11 Q-Q2, BxN; 12 PxB*, with the better game for White.

5 P-K5   ....

In order to drive the Knight from the center and prevent the usual counterstroke ... P-Q4. The defense of the King Pawn by *5 N-B3* ought to give Black the upper hand by the reply *5 ... NxP*. Then, if *6 NxN, P-Q4*. Or if *6 BxPch, KxB*; followed by ... P-Q4.

5 ....   N-N5!

Black cannot employ the usual parry 5 ... P-Q4, as his Bishop rests at K2. Therefore he loses a piece: 5 ... P-Q4?; 6 PxN, PxB; 7 PxB.

The text move is better than 5 ... N-R4 insofar as the Knight bears down on White's King Pawn and is a direct challenge to its existence.

6 **O-O** . . . .

The plausible 6 P-KR3 will not do: 6 P-KR3, B-R5ch; 7 K-B1, N-B7; and Black will be able to capture the Rook and to exit via the loophole at his KN6 square.

The text move seems to promote White's development in as good a way as any. It has been suggested that after 6 N-B3 (instead of 6 O-O), P-Q3; 7 P-Q4, PxP, 8 PxP, QxQch; 9 NxQ, the end game rather favors White, because of his better development.

We take exception to this opinion. After 9 ... B-K3, Black should have no trouble in equalizing. If, for example, 10 BxB, PxB; 11 BxP, O-O, followed by 12 ... N-QB3, Black's development is as good as White's. White's King Pawn, moreover, is at least as much of a target as Black's King Pawn. If, in this line, White interpolates by 11 N-Q4 (instead of 11 BxP), with the idea of picking off Black's King Pawn, Black can defend in different ways. 11 ... B-R5ch, followed by 12 ... K-K2 is one way. 11 ... O-O; 12 NxP, R-B1; 13 BxP,

N-QB3, recovering the Pawn with an easy game, is still another way.

6 .... **P-Q3**

This move successfully collapses White's bridgehead in the center.

7 **PxP** ....

Otherwise, Black threatens to exchange and simplify. Since he enjoys a free and easy development, he ought then to have no problems.

7 .... **QxP**

Black keeps his Bishop at K2 to support a possible ... P-KN4. White will experience difficulty recovering the Pawn.

Black is for choice.

Conclusions and recommendations

The King's Gambit ought to be part of the repertoire of every chessplayer. It does not, however, lead to a forced win for White. It does lead to a stimulating, combinative game, which is the essence of chess, as far as most players are concerned.

Theoretically, Black can equalize or do even better. Practically, the pitfalls for the defender are many—and one of them can be enough!

Chess Movie

TWO PAWNS VERSUS A "PERP"

W<small>HEN</small> English grand master Yates was in a game—win, lose, or draw—his opponent knew that he was going through the wringers. Even Akiba Rubinstein, master of masters, as White, knew it in the following contest, played at Hastings, 1922. The opening: the King's Gambit. It begins *1* P-K4, P-K4; *2* P-KB4, PxP; *3* N-KB3, N-KB3; leading to Diagram 1.

1 The mighty Akiba plays 4 N-B3, and Yates parries with 4 ... P-Q4. White swaps: *5* PxP, NxP; *6* NxN, QxN. The features of the position indicate action. It is unbalanced; White has the extra center Pawn and Black has a free and easy development, his Queen dominantly posted, and a Pawn up.

2 The game continues with *7* P-Q4, B-K2; *8* B-Q3, P-KN4. Rubinstein occupies the center, and Yates defends his material gain. There follows *9* Q-K2, B-KB4; *10* BxB, QxB. Black's strategy is to pare down. For a Pawn plus in the end game is no minor matter, especially in master play.

3 White contrives an ingenious tactic. *11 P-KN4!* is the move. The Pawn is poison, and Black retreats *11 ... Q-Q2*. White continues his development with *12 B-Q2*, and Black keeps pace with *12 ... N-B3*. Both sides castle long: *13 O-O-O, O-O-O*. All is in readiness. The action begins!

4 Rubinstein attempts to shatter Black's Kingside Pawn chain with *14 P-KR4!?* Yates calmly keeps it intact with *14 ... P-B3*. Rubinstein shifts to the center with *15 P-B4*, and Yates bows to his predatory instincts with *15 ... QxNP*. There now follows *16 PxP, PxP*.

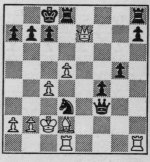

5 *17 P-Q5!* unhinges the Black men from their moorings. Black plays *17 ... N-N5*. And White picks off the Bishop with *18 QxB*. Now Yates comes up with *18 ... N-Q6ch* and will soon recover his piece. There follows *19 K-B2, QxN*. The extra Pawns loom large momentarily.

6 But ho! The master knows what he is doing! There follows *20 Q-K6ch, K-N1; 21 R-R3!* Black must lose a piece after all. Wily Yates fights gamely back. *21 ... QxQRch!* is his answer, and the game continues *22 KxQ, N-B7ch;* forking King and Rook. Has Yates enough in recompense?

7 White plays 23 K-K1, and now Black follows through with 23 ... NxR. White replies 24 QxN, and Black gets his Pawns in motion with 24 ... P-KR4. Then comes 25 B-B3, P-N5; 26 Q-R4, KR-N1. One Pawn must fall. But the others are much closer to the goal. Can they be held?

8 "Take first and look later" is the guiding principle as Rubinstein plays 27 QxRP. Then follows 27 ... P-N6; 28 B-Q4, QR-K1ch; 29 K-Q2, QR-KB1. The situation is uncomfortably warm. Rubinstein attempts a diversion with 30 P-Q6! The scene shifts again. 30 ... PxP is the move.

9 31 Q-R6 follows, looking in the direction of the Black monarch. Yates seeks a haven with 31 ... K-R1. Rubinstein plays 32 QxQP, and Yates checks the immediate danger with 32 ... R-Q1. 33 Q-B5 threatens mate, and Yates continues with RxBch! The denouement is at hand.

10 There follows 34 QxR, P-N7; 35 Q-N1, R-N6. The White King shall not cross the Rubicon. White plays 36 P-N4, and Black makes a loophole with 36 ... P-R3. Then comes 37 K-K2, P-B6ch; and a draw is agreed, for if 38 K-B2, R-R6; 39 Q-Q1, R-R8; 40 Q-Q8ch with perpetual check!

5

A typical King's Gambit Declined position

King's Gambit Declined

CONFLICTING MAXIMS rule the chessboard. "Take first and look later" is one guiding principle, blatantly contradicted by the dictum, "Beware of gifts—Grecian or otherwise." Clearly, chess by maxim leads to quiet confusion.

When material is at stake, instinct favors its appropriation. And with good reason. For *material* is *force*. And a preponderance of force brooks little or no interference or opposition. In theory, the idea behind a capture, even a predatory one, is to build superior reserves in order, if need be, to dole out the booty and maintain the advantage as your opponent loses time in recapturing. In practice, instinct is tempered with judgment. All the factors—time, space, and force—are pitted

41

against each other, and only then is a decision rendered. You have seen this struggle in many a game.

So it is with gambits. Even the simplest of them involves the deepest complexities. It is impossible to determine with certainty that a gain or loss will be offset by some other plus or minus. Consequently, there are those who avoid speculation and decline gambits.

Particularly is this true of the King's Gambit. For White's second move 2 P-KB4, which characterizes the gambit, is double-edged. It aims for pertinent gain but leaves a perceptible weakness in White's Kingside Pawn structure. It is with a view to exploiting that weakness that Black declines the gambit.

Schemes for evading the numerous attacks arising from the King's Gambit were proposed by Lopez as far back as 1561. All in all, about ten lines of play have been tried, most of which have been found wanting. Today, one or two lines are considered good enough to give Black at least equality.

This is the King's Gambit Declined:

1	P-K4	P-K4
2	P-KB4	B-B4

Since Black wishes to maintain the center instead of giving it up by sidetracking his King Pawn, he declines the gambit Pawn. At the same time, he hopes to exploit the weakness created on White's diagonal, KN1-QR7. Now Black's King

Bishop bears on the most vulnerable square in White's King's camp, White's KB2.

Before continuing with the line that develops from Black's second move, it is worth while to digress briefly upon another likely alternative.

There are many other ways for Black to decline the Gambit. Nearly all of them, however, are beset with drawbacks. 2 . . . P-Q3, for instance, leaves Black with a backward development, after 3 N-KB3, N-QB3; 4 P-Q4.

The most aggressive parry to the King's Gambit is 2 . . . P-Q4; known as the Falkbeer Counter Gambit. The main variation of this line runs as follows: 1 P-K4, P-K4; 2 P-KB4, P-Q4; 3 KPxP, P-K5; 4 P-Q3, N-KB3; 5 Q-K2, QxP; 6 N-QB3, B-QN5; 7 B-Q2, BxN; 8 BxB, B-N5; 9 PxP, QxKP; 10 QxQch, NxQ; 11 BxP, R-N1; 12 B-K5, N-QB3; 13 B-Q3, with a better game for White (see diagram below).

DIAGRAM FOR VARIATION

The idea behind the Falkbeer is for Black to ruin White's chances of establishing a strong center and of opening the King Bishop file and the normal diagonal of the Queen Bishop. Black actually succeeds in these aims. For White's King Bishop Pawn stands out like a sore thumb, when it is by-passed by . . . P-K5. But Black's plan costs him a Pawn. Up to the pres-

ent, Black has been unable to show adequate compensation
for the Pawn minus.

The Falkbeer, moreover, is rife with tactical motifs. The
simplest one, for instance, occurs on the third move. Thus,
after *1* P-K4, P-K4; *2* P-KB4, P-Q4; *3* BPxP, White is a dead cock
in the pit: *3* ... Q-R5ch; *4* K-K2, QxKPch; *5* K-B2, B-QB4ch;
6 K-N3, Q-N3ch; etc. If *4* P-N3 (after *3* ... Q-R5ch), QxKPch;
and White loses a Rook.

When, as, and if the Falkbeer is bolstered, it will write
finis to the King's Gambit.

To resume with the main line (from the first diagram):

3 N-KB3 ....

This is probably White's best developing move, since it
puts pressure on Black's center. Any other move might raise
the argument as to whether ... BxN is good or bad for White
—an argument that could not be settled lightly.

It is to be noted that White cannot afford to play *3* PxP??
on account of the reply ... Q-R5ch, which wins at once: thus,
4 P-N3, QxKPch, followed by ... QxR, or *4* K-K2, QxKP mate.

3 .... P-Q3

Defending the King Pawn and making ready for the development of the Queen Bishop.

4 N-B3 ....

A good developing move, bearing on the center.

Alternative lines are no better. For instance, if *4* B-B4, N-KB3; *5* P-Q3, B-K3!; *6* BxB, PxB; *7* PxP, PxP; *8* N-B3, N-B3; *9* B-N5, P-KR3; *10* B-R4, Q-Q3; *11* Q-Q2, O-O-O; *12* O-O-O, P-KN4; *13* B-B2, B-N5; with better attacking prospects for Black.

Or *4* P-B3, N-KB3; *5* PxP, PxP; *6* P-Q4, PxP; *7* PxP, B-N3; *8* P-K5, N-Q4; *9* B-QB4, B-K3; *10* Q-N3, O-O; *11* N-B3, P-QB3; *12* O-O, N-B2; *13* B-K3, N-Q2; with about even chances. White's development is superior; his Pawns are weaker.

4 ....   N-KB3

Black's development goes on apace. The issue is whether White's pressure on the center and the King Bishop file, which will eventually open and accrue to White, will offset Black's command of the long diagonal by his King Bishop and the consequent insecurity to the White monarch.

5 B-B4   ....

White develops according to general principles—first Knights then Bishops.

5 ....   N-B3
6 P-Q3   ....

Development of both sides is nearly completed and the opening assumes a distinctive pattern.

6 ....   B-KN5

Now the threat is ... N-Q5, followed by the capture of White's King Knight and the ensuing breach in White's Kingside Pawn position.

7 P-KR3! ....

Putting the question to the Bishop, before Black has the opportunity of executing his tactical plan.

An alternative but complicated line arises by 7 N-QR4, with a view to getting rid of Black's King Bishop. In that case, Black continues 7 ... N-Q5, and White's position becomes precarious.

7 .... BxN

There is no point to retreating. 7 ... B-KR4? loses a piece after 8 P-KN4, and the retreat in the other direction is clearly a waste of time. White now enjoys a minute material advantage—a Bishop for a Knight.

8 QxB N-Q5

But Black has established an annoying bridgehead in White's camp. Black threatens the Queen and the Queen Bishop Pawn.

9 Q-N3! ....

The retreat, 9 Q-Q1, grants Black a definite superiority in position. In that case, Black continues with ... P-B3, followed

by either … P-Q4 or … P-QN4 and … P-QR4. Perforce
Black gains the upper hand as the position opens up, while
White's King is still in the middle of the board.

By a pointed counterthreat, the text move maintains an
even balance of the position.

9 ….   **Q-K2**

9 … NxPch leads to a powerful attack for White: e.g.,
10 K-Q1, NxR; *11* QxP, R-KB1; *12* PxP, PxP; *13* R-B1, B-K2;
14 B-KN5, etc.

Playable, however, is 9 … PxP and, if *10* QxNP, R-KB1;
11 K-Q1, Q-K2; *12* R-B1, R-KN1; *13* Q-R6, RxP, with a plus
for Black.

10 **PxP**   ….

White opens the King Bishop file and the normal diagonal
of his Queen Bishop and, at the same time, cancels the option
that Black exercises of capturing in Black's good time.

10 ….   **PxP**
11 **K-Q1**   ….

White protects the Queen Bishop Pawn. In doing so, White
forfeits the privilege of castling. *11* B-N3 would mean that
White must part with his Bishop, and he prefers to give up
castling rather than the powerful King Bishop.

11 ….   **P-B3**

With a dual purpose. Now White is denied the use of his
Q5 square, and, at the same time, Black readies for a Queen-
side Pawn demonstration, with the Queen Bishop Pawn serving
as a prop for … P-QN4.

12 **P-QR4**   ….

To prevent the Queen-side Pawn advance, which could
prove embarrassing.

12 ….   **O-O-O**

Black castles long in order to avoid a head-on clash with the opposing forces, waiting for him on the other wing.

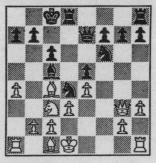

13 **R-B1** . . . .

Not *13* QxNP, KR-N1; *14* QxBP, QxQ; *15* BxQ, RxP, as Black is for choice. White's King position has been penetrated.

The position is about even after *13* R-B1. White's men are better poised for action, with the exception of White's Queen Rook, which cannot join the fray until the White monarch makes way. On the other hand, the slightly unfavorable position of the White King is in Black's favor.

Conclusions and recommendations

The King's Gambit Declined is an excellent psychological weapon against a King's Gambit player. Whereas the player is poised for aggression, he suddenly finds himself in the role of defender—a role that may not suit his style.

As to the actual merits of the Gambit Accepted and the Gambit Declined, they are about on a par.

Chess Movie

ACTIONS SPEAK LOUDER THAN CHECKS

Unabated action from the first move on is the theme of this brilliant King's Gambit Declined. Swedish master Gosta Stoltz (White) picks off a Rook in the opening—with a prayer! —and, by devious defensive plays, manages to contain Rudolph Spielmann's onslaught. Stockholm, 1933, is the scene of play. The game begins: *1* P-K4, P-K4; *2* P-KB4, B-B4; *3* N-KB3, P-Q3; *4* P-B3, P-B4; reaching Diagram No. 1.

1 There follows: 5 BPxP, QPxP; *6* P-Q4, PxQP; *7* B-QB4, PxKP. Each side has indicated a willingness to mix it. Tension reigns supreme as the vulnerable positions of the White and the Black monarchs beckon for enemy incursion. And each opponent is ready to oblige—in a real combat.

2 Stoltz begins the invasion with 8 N-K5, and Spielmann calmly develops *8* ... N-KB3. *9* N-B7 forks Queen and Rook. And Spielmann is unperturbed. *9* ... Q-K2 is his move. There follows *10* NxR, P-Q6. One whole Rook is Spielmann's investment for the position that Black now has.

3 Stoltz pins back the ears of Black's King Knight by *11* B-KN5. Naturally, with a Rook to the good, safety is the first rule, and to swap is the second. Spielmann, however, will die fighting: *11* ... B-B7ch jolts the White King into insecurity. The game then continues: *12* KxB, Q-B4ch.

4 Double attack must recover one piece; and, in the meantime, Spielmann has scored the initial check. White retreats: *13* B-K3, and *13* ... QxKB follows. Now for precaution and development with *14* P-KR3, B-K3; *15* N-Q2, Q-Q4. The question is: can White withstand the coming onslaught?

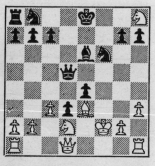

5 White seems unaware, however, that he is being attacked. He thrusts forward: *16* P-KN4, aiming to dislodge one of the props of Black's King Pawn. Then comes *16* ... N-B3; *17* P-B4, Q-Q2; *18* P-N5, B-N5. Black's last is intended to restrain the counterdemonstration.

6 Stoltz swings his Queen to a new focal point. *19* Q-KB1 is the move. Spielmann plays *19* ... B-K7. Stoltz parries with *20* Q-N2, training his sights on the King Pawn. Then comes *20* ... Q-B4ch; *21* K-N1, N-Q2. At last, Black's King Pawn is unguarded. And his attack is now on the wane.

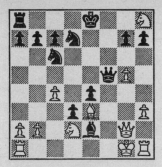

7 22 QxPch is now consequent. There follows 22 ... QxQ; 23 NxQ, K-K2; 24 N-N3, RxN. Black is an exchange behind for a Pawn. But the sting has been removed from his attack. And his Queen Pawn is doomed. The position appears forlorn, and it looks like merely a matter of mopping up.

8 Mopping up it is. 25 NxB begins the operation. Black plays 25 ... PxN, and his isolated King Pawn is the next target. 26 R-R2 practically ends its career. Now follows 26 ... K-B2; 27 RxP, R-K1. Technically, it is all over. Spielmann, however, will not give up the ghost.

9 28 R-Q1 is the move. There is still plenty of resistance in 28 ... N-B1, followed by ... N-K3. But Spielmann plays the natural 28 ... N/Q2-K4. This permits more exchanges. 29 B-B4, R-K3 follow, and Stoltz averts any annoying Knight checks by 30 K-B1. Black continues 30 ... K-N3.

10 31 R-Q5 applies more pressure. Spielmann defends with 31 ... K-B4. Now follows 32 B-N3, and Spielmann stalls with 32 ... R-K2. 33 P-N4 is the finishing touch. The threat is P-N5 to unhinge the support of the King Knight. As this cannot be met, Spielmann resigns.

6

The typical position in Petroff's Defense

Petroff's Defense

Jockeying for control of the center is the sum and substance of the opening goal. Different strategic concepts, however, govern the opening maneuvers: attack and defense, attack and counterattack in the same sector, and attack and counterattack in different fields. The Ruy Lopez, for example, illustrates attack and defense. Black's King Pawn is the fixed target under fire, and a good many of the Black forces are tied to its protection during the early skirmish. The Sicilian, on the other hand, exemplifies independent invasions by both players. There White dominates certain central squares, and Black appropriates other terrain. Petroff's Defense falls in the second category above—attack and counterattack in the same sector.

Perfect symmetry marks Petroff's Defense. After the moves, *1* P-K4, P-K4; *2* N-KB3, Black maintains the balance with *2 . . .* N-KB3. Yet, strangely enough, symmetry does not grant practical equality. Since White moves first, as a rule, White "gets there first." Almost always a position is certain to occur in which Black cannot afford or is not able to emulate White's move. This is the inherent danger of the Petroff.

Despite the theoretical overtones, the Petroff has survived the rigors of the tournament arena for a good many years. One of the oldest defenses to the King Knight Game, it is mentioned in the Gottingen manuscript of 1490. Under the caption, "Two Kings' Knights' Opening," Jaenisch gave it special attention in 1842, and Petroff introduced it into actual play about the same time. Pillsbury, Marshall, and Kashdan have been its champions in more recent times.

The Petroff arises as follows:

1	**P-K4**	**P-K4**
2	**N-KB3**	**N-KB3**

Tit for tat. Attack and counterattack on the invaluable center Pawns.

The prospective exchange of Pawn for Pawn favors the

defender inasmuch as White's King Pawn is the keystone in a mass for aggression as well as a bulwark of defense. The delay involved in effecting the exchange, on the other hand, leaves Black laggard in time, which is translated into superior development for White.

3 NxP   . . . .

Usual. 3 N-B3 transposes into the Four Knights' Game. An indifferent defense, such as 3 P-Q3, has no merit at all as it leads to a cramped position.

A tenable alternative is 3 P-Q4, after which the following line of play might ensue: 3 . . . PxP; 4 P-K5, N-K5; 5 QxP, P-Q4; 6 PxP e.p. NxQP; 7 B-KN5, N-B3!; 8 Q-B3, P-B3; 9 B-KB4, Q-K2ch; 10 B-K2, B-K3; 11 QN-Q2, O-O-O; 12 O-O, Q-B2; with approximately even chances. White's play against the Black monarch on the long side of the board is counterbalanced by Black's possible Pawn demonstration on the other wing.

In this line, special consideration ought to be given to Black's fourth move: . . . N-K5. The tendency of the amateur is to retreat 4 . . . N-N1, or to play 4 . . . N-Q4, where the Knight is not particularly well posted. When projecting a Knight to K5, a vague fear that it may be attacked overcomes the learner.

The alternative line may also follow this course: 3 P-Q4, PxP; 4 P-K5, N-K5; 5 QxP, P-Q4; 6 PxP e.p., NxQP; 7 N-B3, N-B3; 8 Q-KB4, P-KN3!; 9 B-Q2, B-N2; 10 O-O-O, O-O; 11 B-Q3, B-K3; 12 P-KR4, Q-B3—again with equality. Here, oddly enough, White castles long and Black short.

After the text move, White is a Pawn to the good and Black must make every effort to recover it.

Fatal for Black is 3 . . . NxP?; e.g., 4 Q-K2, N-KB3; 5 N-B6 dis ch wins the Queen. Or 3 . . . NxP?; 4 Q-K2, Q-K2; 5 QxN, P-Q3; 6 P-Q4, and White maintains the powerful Pawn plus.

3 . . . .   P-Q3

By first compelling the adverse Knight to move, Black establishes the position to recover the Pawn.

4 **N-KB3**   . . . .

There is no better post for the Knight. 4 N-B4, for instance, interferes with the later development of White's King Bishop. On QB4, the Knight is also vulnerable to future attack.

4 . . . .   **NxP**

Now Black can and must recover the Pawn. Otherwise, he is out a Pawn.

5 **P-Q4**   . . . .

White can maintain symmetry by 5 P-Q3, N-KB3, when he enjoys an infinitesimal plus of the first move. He seeks more, however. His plan is to leave the Black Knight in the advanced post, where it is subject to further attack. In this way, White intends to enhance his development at his opponent's expense.

An alternative frequently encountered at this point is 5 Q-K2. This move attempts to gain development, but involves the exchange of Queens. The line may follow this course: 5 Q-K2, Q-K2; 6 P-Q3, N-KB3; 7 B-N5, QxQch; 8 BxQ, B-K2. White's development is superior, but the absence of Queens cuts down the attacking chances. In the long run, with accurate play, Black equalizes. For White soon reaches his maximum potential and cannot make progress. The onus of accuracy, however, rests with the defender.

5 ....   P-Q4

Also playable is 5 ... B-K2 at once. Black prefers, however, to expand the diagonal of his King Bishop. The omission of ... P-Q4 can conceivably lead to a cramped game as it grants White the opportunity to play P-Q5 and usurp a large chunk of terrain.

6 B-Q3   ....

While the attack on the projected Knight seems meaningless at the present, it is a prelude to a future plan to unhinge its support by an eventual P-QB4.

6 ....   B-Q3

Black follows suit. Note that the position is symmetrical, except that Black's Knight at K5 is a theoretical target. Contrariwise, if the Knight can be maintained on its present square, it may serve as a base for incursion into White's domain.

Black may avoid symmetry and lead to interesting play by 6 ... B-K2. Then the game may take the following course: 6 ... B-K2; 7 O-O, N-QB3!; 8 P-B4, N-QN5; 9 PxP, NxB; 10 QxN, QxP; 11 R-K1, B-KB4; 12 N-B3, NxN; 13 QxN, P-QB3; 14 R-K5, Q-Q2; 15 P-Q5!, O-O; 16 PxP, PxP; with equality.

This line, however, is extremely tricky and places a premium on accuracy.

7 O-O   O-O

Development goes on apace.

8 P-B4   ....

First step in the plan to unhinge the Knight.

8 ....   P-QB3

Supplying a prop.

Marshall's favored line was 8 ... B-KN5. But it involves the sacrifice of two Pawns for a dangerous attack. When played by Marshall, the whole idea was little explored, and the U.S. champion scored many notable successes with it. Current analysis, however, has shorn the line of its terror. The line may pursue the following course: 8 ... B-KN5; 9 PxP, P-KB4;

10 N-B3, (or A), N-Q2; *11* P-KR3, B-R4; *12* NxN, PxN; *13*
BxP, N-B3; *14* B-B5, K-R1; *15* P-KN4, NxQP; *16* B-K6, and
Black has insufficient compensation for his material minus.
The excellent squares K5 and N5 beckon the White Knight,
and this more than makes up for White's shaky King-side
position.

(A) Not *10* R-K1?, BxPch; *11* KxB, NxP; *12* Q-K2, NxB;
13 QxN, BxN; *14* QxB, Q-R5ch; followed by *15* ... QxR.
(This is Marshall's trap, in which this writer had the unfortunate experience to fall.)

9 R-K1   ....

With the idea of continuing pressure on the target Knight,
while gaining development.

Alternative lines lead to no advantage. If *9* N-B3, for instance, *9* ... NxN; *10* PxN, B-KN5; *11* P-KR3, B-R4; *12* PxP,
PxP; *13* Q-N3, BxN; *14* QxNP, N-Q2; *15* PxB, N-N3; *16* R-N1,
Q-B3; and Black's sounder Pawn skeleton compensates for
his material minus.

Or *9* Q-B2, N-R3!; *10* BxN, PxB; *11* QxP, R-K1; *12* Q-R4,
QxQ; *13* NxQ, N-N5; *14* N-R3, R-K5; *15* N-B3, B-N5; and
Black's position is superior despite the momentary Pawn minus.

9 ....   R-K1

Maintaining the advanced post.

10 N-B3   ....

There is no good way of placing additional pressure on the
Knight. Consequently, White must permit simplification.

10 ....   NxN

To maintain the Knight on its advanced post by *10* ...
P-KB4 is perilous. Then White continues with *11* PxP and
attempts to exploit the weakness created on Black's long diagonal (KN1-QR7) by Q-N3.

11 RxRch   ....

If *11* PxN, RxRch; *12* QxR. White is somewhat better off with his Queen on Queen square than on King square.

11	**QxR**
12 **PxN**	**B-KN5**

Black's men are a bit more aggressively posted, though White still leads in development and enjoys a better Pawn position.

13 **B-Q2** ....

Now White threatens *14* BxPch, KxB; *15* N-N5ch, followed by the recovery of the piece—not possible on the previous move on account of Black's mate at K8.

13 .... **Q-Q1**

To prevent the threat, while gaining future access for the Queen to KB3 or QB2 or N3 or R4. Any Pawn move, such as *13* ... P-KR3, weakens the King-side Pawn structure.

14 **R-N1** ....

Seizing the open file with a view to exploiting the lead in development.

14 .... **PxP**

A necessary interpolation. After the following move, Black

can defend himself by ... Q-B2, without allowing White to execute his earlier threat of BxPch.

15 **BxP**　　　　**Q-B2**

White's position is slightly preferable.

Conclusions and recommendations

Since most lines of the Petróff lead to a somewhat symmetrical position, with White having a move in hand, the prospects for Black are none too inviting. In any one of the alternative variations at White's disposal, moreover, the onus of accuracy falls upon Black. This, coupled with the fact that Marshall's line has been shorn of its sting, rates the Petroff below par—unless, of course, Marshall's variation can be bolstered.

Chess Movie

GIVEAWAY CHESS

W HEN TWO disciples of the art of sacrifice in chess meet
over the chessboard, the result ought to be "giveaway" chess.
It is. First Marshall gives up a couple of Pawns, then Spielmann gives up three. Then Marshall gives up the exchange
and keeps giving until mate. The scene: Hamburg, 1910. The
game begins with *1* P-K4, P-K4; *2* N-KB3, N-KB3; *3* NxP,
P-Q3; *4* N-KB3, NxP (see first diagram). Marshall is Black.

1 The game continues
with the usual *5* P-Q4,
P-Q4; *6* B-Q3, B-Q3.
Marshall more or less dupli-
cates his opponent's moves.
Here, however, the players get
off on a new tack. Spielmann
plays *7* O-O, and Marshall
follows with *7* ... B-KN5.
Both Black Bishops are di-
rected against White's King.

2 Spielmann attempts to
unhinge the advanced
Knight with *8* P-B4,
and Marshall "sacs" a Pawn
with *8* ... O-O. Then comes
9 PxP, P-KB4; *10* N-B3, N-
Q2. A second Pawn is prof-
fered. What are a couple of
Pawns, when the enemy King
is at stake? That is the idea,
and only time can test it.

3 First Spielmann plays *11* P-KR3, now driving the opposing Bishop. After *11* ... B-R4, he continues with *12* NxN, PxN; *13* BxP, picking off the second Pawn. Marshall goes on nonchalantly with *13* ... N-B3, and the picture clarifies. White's Bishop will move, and so his Pawn structure weakens.

4 Spielmann plays *14* B-B5, indirectly defending his Queen Pawn, and Marshall gets out of the line of check by *14* ... K-R1. Now follows *15* P-KN4, NxQP. White has been compelled to overexpand his King-side Pawns. But then he has a Pawn plus to salve the pain of any coming abuse.

5 Spielmann falters. *16* Q-Q3 is his move. Now Marshall lets fly a sockdolager. *16* ... N-N5 puts the White Queen to rout. Spielmann follows with *17* Q-K4, and the game continues: *17* ... B-B2; *18* B-N5, Q-K1. Marshall offers a friendly exchange of Queens. That is, if you want to call it friendly!

6 Spielmann disdains the offer with *19* N-K5. He will rue the day. Marshall lets go another humdinger, with *19* ... B-Q4, compelling a retreat. There follows *20* Q-K2, N-B3. One Pawn has already come home, and now the powerful pin brings glad tidings of the other. Is more to come besides?

7 21 Q-Q3 is Spielmann's move. He wishes to salvage whatever he can out of the coming melee. The game continues: 21 ... NxN; 22 PxN, QxP, threatening mate. Spielmann tosses this off easily with 23 Q-KN3, and Marshall picks off another Pawn, with 23 ... QxP for a Pawn to the good.

8 Spielmann replies with 24 Q-R4. Now he's threatening a little mate, too. Marshall won't waste time retreating or advancing his Pawns. 24 ... RxB is the move! When Marshall gives, he gives full measure. Spielmann then captures with 25 PxR, and Marshall's inevitable sequel is 25 ... Q-K4.

9 This mate isn't so easy to thwart. Spielmann tries 26 Q-N3, and so Marshall now plucks off yet another Pawn, 26 ... QxP. Spielmann pleads for an exchange with 27 Q-N4, but Marshall is adamant. He returns: 27 ... Q-K4. There follows 28 KR-K1, Q-R7ch. White's King must march.

10 29 K-B1 is Spielmann's move, and Marshall plays 29 ... R-KB1, again menacing mate. This time it isn't easy to parry either. White runs for the open with 30 K-K2. He is cut down in his tracks with 30 ... QxPch; 31 K-Q3, P-N4. Facing threats from all directions, Spielmann resigns.

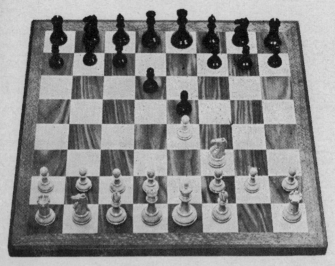

7

The typical position at the outset of Philidor's Defense

Philidor's Defense

THE SIMPLE WAY is not always the best way. Ready riposte is its goal, while long-term considerations are discounted lightly.

So it is with the Philidor. In the delicate thrusts and parries revolving about center control, which constitute the opening skirmish, Black employs an easy expedient. After the moves *1* P-K4, P-K4; *2* N-KB3, he defends his King Pawn with the simple *2 . . .* P-Q3. His plan is to hold the strong point at his K4 square not by devious, tortuous maneuvers, but by straightforward defense. This is all well and good—as far as it goes. It does not, however, go far enough. For one thing, it frees White instantly to play P-Q4—whereas the usual course compels the first player to resort to intricate stratagems before he can successfully enforce this move. In turn, this means that the pressure on Black's center mounts rapidly, and Black is reduced to a doubly defensive cramped position. Black's second move, moreover, obstructs the development of his King Bishop. This fault is negligible since Black often posts his King Bishop on the second rank. By no stretch of the imagination, however, can it be considered a virtue.

Philidor's Defense was first noticed in the Gottingen manuscript (1490). It gains its name from the celebrated French player, François André Danican Philidor, who remodeled and popularized it.*

Today, it is occasionally adopted to steer the play away from routinized channels. Late world champion Alekhine sometimes gave it a fling—using the modernized Hanham Variation. In the main, its prospects may be summarized as expressed in the first line of a poem: "The Philidor is a horrible bore."

It may, however, win games!

The Philidor arises as follows:

1	P-K4	P-K4
2	N-KB3	P-Q3

As a rule, when 1 P-K4 is met by 1 ... P-K4, White's plan is to put mounting pressure on Black's King Pawn, until it is dislodged. When and if it gives way, White intends to usurp the center.

Black, on the other hand, places as many obstacles—tactical and strategical—in White's way as he can. With perfect defense, the struggle for the center is a standoff, and the players then direct their efforts to other fields.

Perfect defense for Black calls for counterthreats sufficient to prevent White from successfully enforcing an early P-Q4.

* According to Chernev and Reinfeld in *The Fireside Book of Chess*, Philidor never played the defense named after him. For one thing, he practically always gave odds! But he did present and recommend a line in that defense in his famous book, *Analyze du Jeu des Échecs*.

For, when White's Queen Pawn engages Black's King Pawn, the pressure rises to such an extent that Black is soon compelled to swap. Then White remains with a dominating King Pawn as against a backward Queen Pawn for Black, and White virtually controls the center.

Black's efforts, therefore, are bent upon preventing an adverse P-Q4. In the Philidor, this is not the case, and, consequently, Black practically concedes the center. In turn, this means that his development will be retarded and backward.

In order not to confuse the issue, it should be noted that in many openings, such as the Scotch and Center Game, White can and does play an early P-Q4. The situation, however, is not analogous. For, in these openings, Black always gets some compensation for White's impetuosity. The compensation may be no more than a tempo. But it is compensation.

The text move permits, even provokes, the adverse P-Q4 and gains nothing in return. On this account, it is deficient.

It is also deficient, to a lesser extent, in that it limits the mobility of the King Bishop.

3 P-Q4 . . . .

The natural continuation. The idea is to force Black to play . . . PxP. In that case, White's King Pawn dominates a good portion of the center by commanding vital squares on the fifth rank, while its counterpart, Black's Queen Pawn, ineffectually touches only the fourth rank.

3 . . . . N-Q2

Black must maintain his King Pawn at all cost. 3 . . . N-QB3 will not do; for after 4 PxP, PxP; 5 QxQch, Black either loses a Pawn or forfeits the privilege of castling. The Knight on Q2, moreover, allows for the construction of an interesting Pawn array, which is to serve as a barrier against invasion as well as a prop for a possible counterattack later on.

4 B-QB4 . . . .

The Bishop aims at the most vulnerable point in Black's camp—his KB2 square.

4 .... **P-QB3**

The purpose of this move is threefold: To begin with, it clears the square QB2, so that it may be occupied by Black's Queen, whence it must protect Black's King Pawn. Then the move foreshadows a future Queen-side demonstration based on ... P-QN4–P-QR4 and a general expansion on the Queen's wing. Lastly, the move guards Black's Q4 square so that no opposing man can penetrate with facility.

Note that 4 ... B-K2? loses a Pawn at once: e.g., 5 PxP, NxP; 6 NxN, PxN; 7 Q-R5, threatening simultaneously the King Pawn and the King Bishop Pawn. After 4 ... B-K2?; 5 PxP, PxP; then 6 Q-Q5 wins.

The maneuver ... P-QB3 and ... Q-B2 is part and parcel of a system worked out and introduced into tournament practice by Major Hanham. The variation under discussion is therefore referred to as the Hanham Variation.

White's next move is a good way to continue development, although alternative moves, such as 5 N-B3 are also tenable. An interesting idea here is 5 PxP, PxP; 6 BxPch, KxB; 7 NxPch. White gets a powerful attack, but it can be rebuffed by proper defense.

5 **O-O** . . . .

Another try is 5 N-N5. Then the line might run as follows: 5 ... N-R3; 6 O-O, N-N3!; 7 B-N8, B-K2; 8 Q-R5, O-O; and Black is able to hold the position with precision defense.

One misstep in the above line can be fatal. For example, if 5 N-N5, N-R3; 6 O-O, B-K2?; 7 N-K6!, PxN; 8 BxN, N-N3; 9 BxNP, and White wins because of the uncomfortable position of the Black monarch. In this line, 8 ... PxB?; 9 Q-R5ch, and White soon mates.

Finally, Alekhine recommended 5 P-QR4, after ... P-QB3 (as in his game against Marco) to prevent ... P-QN4 once and for all.

5 . . . . **B-K2**

Here again, Black can falter: 5 ... KN-B3?; 6 PxP, KNxP; 7 PxP, QN-B3; 8 R-K1, and Black is in trouble. There are even pitfalls within the pitfalls. For example, if 5 ... KN-B3?; 6 PxP, QNxP; 7 NxN, PxN; 8 BxPch, and Black is out a Pawn. Or 5 ... KN-B3?; 6 PxP, PxP; 7 N-N5, and Black cannot hold the King Bishop Pawn.

It is quite possible White's strongest line is now 6 PxP, PxP; 7 N-N5!, BxN; 8 Q-R5, P-KN3; 9 QxB, QxQ; 10 BxQ, and White has the advantage of the two Bishops.

6 N-B3 . . . .

The text move, however, maintains the character of the game, insofar as it does not drive for an immediate end game, even a favorable one.

6 . . . . KN-B3

At last, after avoiding the traps and stratagems, Black is able to bring out all his King-side men.

7 P-QR4 . . . .

This move is unusual, but pointed. Eventually, White contemplates action on the other wing. For the moment he therefore stifles any counterplay on the Queen-side. This would be possible if Black got in . . . P-QN4-5. For the Pawn advance would dispossess White's Queen Knight and leave White's King Pawn unguarded.

7 . . . . P-KR3

Usual here is 7 ... O-O. Then White gets the better game by perfectly routine moves. The following is an example from the game Alekhine–Marco, Stockholm, 1912: 7 ... O-O; 8 Q-K2, P-KR3; 9 B-N3, Q-B2; 10 P-R3, K-R2; 11 B-K3, P-KN3; 12 QR-Q1, K-N2; 13 N-KR2, N-KN1; 14 P-B4.

Observe the Hanham idea in this line—Black's Queen at the QB2 square to maintain the center.

The text move conceals its real purpose. It is not to prevent the adverse B-KN5, as appears at first sight. Instead, it is intended as a prelude to a King-side assault, with the Rook Pawn serving as a prop for the later advance ... P-KN4. This plan, in conjunction with the maneuver ... N-B1-N3 has the makings of a formidable assault in view.

8 P-QN3!   ....

The idea here is to fianchetto the Queen Bishop, which then exerts indirect pressure on Black's King Pawn.

Against normal developing moves, Black is able to obtain equal chances. A game Alexander–Fine continued as follows: 8 B-R2, P-KN4; 9 PxP, PxP; 10 Q-K2, B-Q3; 11 R-Q1, Q-K2; 12 B-K3, N-B4; 13 N-Q2, N-K3. Black's prospects are good.

8 ....   Q-B2

Indirectly protecting the King Pawn, which will be under attack in the immediate future. On general principles, when a Queen is relegated to defending a Pawn, something is chronically wrong!

9 B-N2   ....

Nimzovich–Marco, Gothenburg, 1920, continued as follows: 9 ... N-B1?; 10 PxP, PxP; 11 NxP!, QxN; 12 N-Q5!, Q-Q3; 13 B-R3, PxN (13 ... P-B4 14 P-K5!); 14 BxQ—in favor of White.

9 ... N-B1?, however, is a blunder. Better is 9 ... O-O. Even then White's position is superior.

Conclusions and recommendations

The one variation of the Philidor that has enjoyed even slight favor in tournament practice is the Hanham. Practically, it is self-condemned, per se, since it relegates a Queen to the menial task of guarding a Pawn, which *may* be attacked.

Despite the numerous pitfalls and dour prospects that exist for the defender, the Philidor is worth an occasional fling against a player who is oblivious of its proper course. The execution of Black's plan, unmolested, leaves him, strangely enough, with the upper hand.

Chess Movie

A FLAILING PHILIDOR

SIMULTANEOUS attack and defense is the order of the following sparkling classic. Both Kings are exposed to flailing blows from all directions. Finally, Hungarian master Breyer sets up a series of irresistible checks, and the immovable White King of Havasi is moved to resignation. Budapest, 1917, is the scene of play. The game begins with *1* P-K4, P-K4; *2* N-KB3, P-Q3; *3* P-Q4, N-Q2; *4* B-QB4, P-QB3.

1 There follows *5* O-O, B-K2; *6* N-B3, Q-B2; *7* B-K3, P-KR3. White is making the usual routine moves, and Black is contemplating an assault against the opposing monarch. His intentions, however, are well concealed. For who would suspect the puny ... P-KR3 as packing a wallop?

2 White prepares the advance of his King Bishop Pawn by *8* N-Q2, and Black signals the attack with *8* ... P-KN4. Immediately, White swings his other Knight to the King-side with *9* N-K2, and Black follows suit. *9* ... N-B1 is his move. Now follows *10* N-KN3, N-N3. All is yet serene.

3 White is first to enter with *11* N-B5. Black parries with *11* ... P-Q4. White retreats *12* B-Q3, and Black swaps *12* ... BxN. White recaptures *13* PxB, and Black now enters *13* ... N-B5. The opposing maneuvers are along the same line, except that Black knows where the White King lives!

4 There follows *14* BxN, KPxB; *15* R-K1, O-O-O. Black's abode is on the other side. White now readies for an onslaught against the Black King and prepares with *16* P-QB3. Black brings out the rest of his forces with *16* ... N-B3. This is the proverbial calm before the storm.

5 *17* P-QN4 is White's way of instituting the attack. The race is on. Black plays *17* ... P-N5. There follows *18* R-N1, B-Q3; *19* Q-R4, P-B6. Each side is poised for action against the enemy King. The same old question obtains: "Who will get there first with the most?" Only time will tell.

6 White builds a barrier with *20* P-N3, which Black immediately sets out to breach with *20* ... P-KR4. White counters with *21* P-N5, and it appears that he has arrived. Black plays *21* ... P-R5. It all seems so slow. Now comes *22* PxBP, PxNP. With one fell move, all fury is loosened!

7 White attempts to consolidate with 23 RPxP. His attack can wait for a move. *But it can't.* Black replies 23 ... BxP!; and White's King position is deftly penetrated. 24 RxP is White's move, and 24 ... BxPch is Black's bombastic reply. Checks must be respected, and so Black has the lead.

8 White captures 25 KxB, and Black closes in with 25 ... Q-R7ch. White attempts to exit with 26 K-K3, and black keeps the King in place with 26 ... Q-R3ch. Black dare not let up. If he fails to give check, he will be on the receiving end. And not for long. For White's checks can be deadly.

9 White retreats with 27 K-B2, and Black captures 27 ... QxNch. Always with check! White plays 28 R-K2. Perhaps this will compel a respite. But no, Black pitches everything at his command into the fray. 28 ... N-K5ch is the move. There is no letup, for Black can't afford one.

10 29 BxN is forced, and Black answers with 29 ... QxRch. The material gain is only incidental. The King is the target. White plays 30 K-N3, and Black continues with 30 ... Q-R7ch. More checks. It is impossible to avoid the checks. In fact, it is impossible to avoid mate. White resigns.

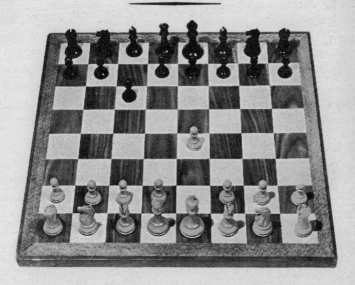

8

The typical position in the Caro-Kann Defense

Caro-Kann Defense

Every chess opening revolves about the play in the center. This ties up with the ultimate goal of the debut, which is to usurp the vital terrain so that the opponent, limited as it were to marginal squares, will be at a disadvantage. By virtue of his first move, White is first to drive a stake into the center. And Black is faced with a problem. Shall he follow suit on adjacent squares or shall he attempt to undermine his adversary's claim?

The problem is clear cut. But its solution leads to multifarious byways, each, in turn, with many ramifications ending in a plus or minus.

Out of this maze comes the Caro-Kann, another way of challenging White's birthright—the initial move. It is nothing more than a solid attempt by the defender to set up a well-fortified stake of his own in the center—or, failing that, to yield Pawn control of the center in return for a free and easy development.

The Caro-Kann is an ancient defense, mentioned by Polerio in 1590. Originally, however, Black's play was so badly man-handled that the defense was snugly tucked away for many years. Later, it was introduced into modern play by Kann of Pesth and practiced by Caro of Berlin. Hence the name.

Though not played too frequently, the Caro-Kann does crop up regularly today; so any *1* P-K4 player must know it.

It is generally considered a safe though dull defense. Some of its disciples, however, may be noted as in the top fringe of the chess fraternity, among them Capablanca, Nimzovich, and Flohr.

The Caro-Kann arises as follows:

1 **P-K4**   **P-QB3**
(See photo)

Black's first move characterizes the Caro-Kann. Of the two moves, however, White's is clearly the better. For his Pawn strikes at the vital central terrain, whereas Black's is merely a prop for what is to follow. But this is not the true criterion of values. Future prospects must also be weighed. After Black's next play, a fairer comparison can be made.

Black's move inaugurates a series of patterns—depending upon White's replies. Each of these patterns has something in Black's favor. In general, the move is a forerunner to a direct challenge in the center. Noteworthy is the fact that Black is able to develop his Queen Bishop—contrasting favorably with the French Defense in which that critter is locked in.

2 **P-Q4**   . . . .

This is probably White's best move, though by no means his only one. 2 N-QB3 leads to interesting and trappy lines. For example, 2 N-QB3, P-Q4; 3 N-B3, PxP; 4 NxP, B-B4; 5 N-N3, B-N3; 6 P-KR4, P-KR3; 7 N-K5, B-R2; 8 Q-R5, P-KN3; 9 B-B4!, and White is definitely for choice.

Black may play 4 . . . B-N5, however, instead of 4 . . . B-B4. In that event, White gains a minimal advantage with 5 P-KR3, BxN; 6 QxB. He has the two Bishops.

$$2 \ldots \ldots \qquad \text{P-Q4}$$

To challenge the center.

3 N-QB3   . . . .

Here White concentrates on bringing out his forces rapidly, while bearing on the center. Other lines are also tenable.

One line in particular, known as the Panov-Botvinnik Attack, has enjoyed considerable popularity. It runs as follows: 3 PxP, PxP; 4 P-QB4, N-KB3; 5 N-QB3, N-B3; 6 B-N5, PxP; 7 P-Q5, N-K4; 8 Q-Q4, N-Q6ch; 9 BxN, PxB; 10 N-B3, and White leads in development and prospects.

In playing the Panov-Botvinnik, however, White must be prepared to accept an isolated Queen Pawn. Thus, if 6 . . . P-K3 (instead of 6 . . . PxP); the game may take the following course: 7 N-B3, PxP; 8 BxP. Here, too, the advantage in space overshadows the chronic weakness of the isolated Pawn. But the onus of capitalizing on that extra space falls upon White. Should he fail to make that good, his ending will, indeed, be difficult.

Another continuation is 3 PxP, PxP; 4 B-Q3. This simplifying plan is based on aggressive considerations. White hopes to poise his men for attack against the Black King, while he checks Black's aspirations on the other side of the board. Note that White will control the half-opened King file, while Black possesses the half-opened Queen Bishop file.

In practice, however, White's assault in this line can be contained, and Black's demonstration on the other wing can become a real menace. The game may go as follows: 4 ... N-QB3; 5 P-QB3, N-B3; 6 B-KB4, B-N5; 7 N-B3, P-K3; 8 Q-N3, Q-B1; 9 QN-Q2, B-K2.

Still another interesting try is 3 P-KB3. It is an effort to maintain Pawn control of the center—or, in the event of an exchange of Pawns, to open lines for a fierce attack. For example, 3 ... PxP; 4 PxP, P-K4; 5 N-KB3, PxP; 6 B-QB4, B-K2; 7 O-O, N-B3; 8 N-N5, O-O; 9 NxBP, RxN; 10 BxRch, KxB; 11 P-K5, K-N1; 12 PxN, BxP; 13 N-Q2, B-K3; 14 N-K4, and White has the better game (Teichman–Mieses, 1913).

On the other hand, Black need not fall in line with White's plan. He may continue quietly with 3 ... P-K3 and attempt to exploit the weakness inherent in White's advance of the King Bishop Pawn: 3 ... P-K3; 4 B-K3, Q-N3; 5 N-Q2, N-Q2; 6 B-Q3, P-QB4; 7 P-B3, P-B5; 8 B-QB2, QxNP; 9 N-K2, Q-R6; 10 O-O, N-N3; 11 PxP, PxP; 12 R-K1, B-Q2.

Black decides to yield the center, for he is at a loss for any good temporizing move. By ridding himself of White's King Pawn, however, he has created a square for his Queen Bishop at his KB4.

Position after 3 N-QB3

3 ....   PxP

Any other move, such as *3 ... N-B3;* invites perilous complications: on *3 ... N-B3; 4 P-K5, N-Q2; 5 P-K6,* for example, the sacrifice of the Pawn opens lines leading directly to the Black monarch. The defense is difficult, if not hopeless.

4 NxP   ....

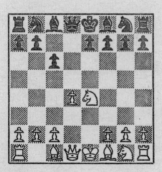

4 ....   B-B4

An alternative, difficult for both sides, is *4 ... N-B3.* After *5 NxNch,* Black suffers from a poorer Pawn position: e.g., *5 ... KPxN; 6 B-QB4, B-K2; 7 Q-R5!, O-O; 8 N-K2, P-KN3; 9 Q-B3, R-K1; 10 B-KR6, B-KB4; 11 O-O-O, B-K5; 12 Q-QN3,* and White's prospects for both middle game and end game are superior. The extra Pawn on the Queen-side is a determining factor in the end game.

After *4 ... N-B3; 5 NxNch, NPxN*, Black has the inferior game. See the Chess Movie on page 84.

4 ... P-K3 does not commend itself as it shuts in Black's Queen Bishop. And *4 ... N-Q2*—to prepare ... KN-B3 without risk of doubled Pawns—may be met by *5 N-KB3, KN-B3; 6 N-N3*. In this line, White retains his edge in terrain and favorable disposition of forces and can aim, as a last resort, at utilizing his Queen-side Pawn majority in the end game.

The text is part and parcel of the Caro-Kann in that the Queen Bishop obtains a satisfactory development.

5 N-N3 . . . .

This move gains a vital tempo—unless Black wishes to concede "the two Bishops."

Instead, White could essay a gambit with *5 B-Q3*, and, after *5 ... QxP; 6 N-KB3*, have a tremendous lead in development. That this is sufficient for the Pawn, however, is another story—even though many of the giants of chessdom have experimented successfully with the idea.

5 . . . . **B-N3**

Black remains on the strong diagonal.

6 **N-B3** . . . .

This veers from *Practical Chess Openings* in which *6* P-KR4 is given. The sequence above is slightly better insofar as Black is now compelled to play accurately—on his own! Otherwise he may oblige by meeting White's plan (see next note) half-way.

6 . . . .   N-Q2

On the natural *6* ... N-B3, White's plan leaps to life with *7* P-KR4, P-KR3; *8* N-K5 (gaining a tempo by threatening to capture the Bishop and so disrupt Black's Pawn structure), B-R2; *9* B-QB4, P-K3; *10* Q-K2 (threatening *11* NxBP with a crushing assault).

The text move forestalls N-K5.

7 B-QB4   . . . .

Practical Chess Openings may now be reached by trans-position with 7 P-KR4, P-KR3; *8* P-R5, B-R2; *9* B-Q3, BxB; *10* QxB, P-K3; *11* B-Q2, KN-B3; *12* O-O-O, B-Q3; *13* QR-K1, BxN; *14* PxB, O-O; *15* R-R4, and White is for choice.

The text move is played on the theory that since White is the aggressor, he ought to maintain his forces for the attack rather than submit to exchange (as by 7 B-Q3). If he can post his pieces to bear in the direction of the opposing mon-arch, so much the better.

An alternative is 7 N-R4, gaining the minimal advantage of Bishop for Knight.

$$7 \dots \qquad \textbf{P-K3}$$

To limit the scope of White's King Bishop.

$$8 \textbf{ Q-K2} \qquad \dots$$

White is for choice. A good plan for future action is O-O, followed by the development of the Queen Bishop, posting a Rook on the Queen file and then the retreat of the King Bishop to QN3, making way for P-QB4. It is not easy for Black to meet this proposed action.

Conclusions and recommendations

The Caro-Kann is inherently deficient since Black must sacrifice his foothold in the center in order to gain a facile development. With correct play, all lines lead to a plus for White. Despite this, White's edge is of such a minimal nature, a misstep may easily throw the advantage the other way. On this ground, and also for the sake of variety, the Caro-Kann can be recommended.

Chess Movie

CRIME FAILS AGAIN

CLASSICAL punishment for violations of long-tested principles is the motif in this Caro-Kann. When Salo Flohr (Black) neglects his strategic ABC's, I. A. Horowitz launches a punitive expedition. The result is an impressive triumph for sound, imaginative chess. The game (U.S.A.–U.S.S.R. Radio Match, 1945) opens: *1* P-K4, P-QB3; *2* P-Q4, P-Q4; *3* N-QB3, PxP; *4* NxP, N-B3; *5* NxNch, NPxN (see Diagram 1).

1 White now signals aggressive intentions by *6* N-K2. Flohr will not be permitted to relax with a humdrum variation! The game continues: *6* ... B-B4; *7* N-N3, B-N3; *8* P-KR4, P-KR3; *9* P-R5, B-R2; *10* P-QB3, Q-N3; *11* B-QB4, N-Q2; *12* P-R4! Now castling on *either* side is risky for Black!

2 Alarmed by the threat of a crippling advance of the White Queen Rook Pawn, Flohr blocks that with *12* ... P-R4. There follows: *13* Q-B3, P-K3; *14* O-O. Horowitz has an ideal setup, while Flohr's pieces lack coordination. Black switches his Queen Bishop to a better diagonal by *14* ... B-B7.

3 White continues developing with *15* B-B4, and Black pursues his plan, replying *15* ... B-N6. The next moves are: *16* B-Q3, P-K4; *17* B-K3, B-Q4; *18* B-K4, Q-N6. Black is getting nowhere fast. He has lost time; his King is insecure; and his men are still awkwardly deployed.

4 And matters are rapidly coming to a head: *19* PxP, PxP; *20* QR-Q1, BxB; *21* QxB, Q-K3; *22* R-Q2. Every move by Horowitz underscores the defects of Flohr's game. Soon the Russian will be left without plausible ideas. Flohr tries *22* N-B3, and Horowitz plays *23* Q-B3.

5 Unable to unite his Rooks, Black at least takes a file: *23* ... KR-N1. White's *24* KR-Q1 now trains heavy siege guns on the Black King. The threat is *25* N-B5. Black seeks to stop it with *24* ... R-N5? *25* N-B5!! anyway. But how will White meet the next move?—*25* ... P-K5.

6 White's threat was *26* N-Q6ch or *26* R-Q6. With his Queen attacked, however, White has no time for this. Apparently, he must lose a piece. But his next move reveals the brilliancy in the position. He lunges *26* B-N6! He threatens mate at Q8—and Black is left without any sound resource.

7 Flohr makes the best of a bad business: 26 ... RxPch. What follows is easily understandable: 27 QxR, QxN; 28 R-Q8ch, RxR; 29 RxRch, K-K2. Now precision chess—*30 Q-N3!*—deprives Black of any last-minute chance for a swindle. Mate is again threatened, and Black's reply is virtually forced.

8 For a split second, *30 ... N-Q2* holds White at bay. But the kill is not far off. White presses on with *31 B-B7*, renewing the mating threat. Note the futility of Black's Bishop In effect, White may almost be said to be a Rook ahead! The game now continues with *31 ... Q-Q4; 32 P-QB4, Q-KN4.*

9 With a won ending, Horowitz cheerfully exchanges Queens. There's not much left: *33 QxQch, PxQ; 34 R-R8, K-K3; 35 BxP, P-KB4; 36 B-B3, P-B5.* The Black Pawn moves represent the final twitches of a moribund position. Elementary care is all that is needed now to deliver the quietus.

10 There follows: *37 P-R5, P-N5; 38 P-N4, P-B6; 39 B-Q2*, and White's King Rook Pawn is primed to race on for a touchdown. Black therefore plays *39 ... K-B2.* The lethal blow, *40 R-R7*, promptly follows; and, when *40 ... P-N6* is answered by *41 RxP*, Flohr resigns. A fine didactic game.

9

The typical position in the Nimzo-Indian

Nimzo-Indian Defense

Strange as it may seem, this defense which is rooted in a theoretical fallacy, enjoys a large share of success and, in fact, is the current leaning post of the majority of masters. After the moves, *1* P-Q4, N-KB3; *2* P-QB4, P-K3; *3* N-QB3, Black resorts to an early sortie with his King Bishop by playing *3* ... B-N5, setting up a pin.

Such a speedy pin of the Knight, as a general rule, is justifiable only insofar as it exerts indirect pressure on the center. By nullifying the scope of the beleaguered "critter," the pin in turn cuts off its command of the mid-section of the playing field.

So far, so good. The Bishop move achieves its main purpose. There is, however, another consideration. What is to become of the Bishop during the future course of the game, particularly when it is under attack? Will it retreat or will it capture the Knight?

When a *King* Knight is thus pinned, a Pawn assault on the Bishop weakens the position of the King. When a Queen Knight is pinned, the consequence of a Pawn assault is not the same. The King does not enter into the reckoning, and the advanced Pawns dominate important terrain, which fact overshadows the weakness innate in the advance. *Ergo*, in the Nimzo-Indian, when, as, and if Black's King Bishop is attacked, say, by P-QR3, it is committed to the swap ... BxN. Since a Bishop is definitely, though minutely, more valuable than a Knight—Q. E. D.—Black's policy is inept.

On the surface then, the Nimzo-Indian ought to be a losing game. In its favor, however, is one modifying clause. White often winds up with an awkward Pawn cluster on his left wing. That this is sufficient compensation for the exchange of Bishop for Knight is dubious. Yet up to the present the success of the Nimzo-Indian remains unchallenged. And nothing succeeds like success.

The Nimzo-Indian is a product of the Queen's Indian Defense, patterned by the late grand master Aron Nimzovich. Under the rules that prevailed in India years ago, a Pawn could move only one square at a time—never two squares. Hence fianchetto developments were popular, and these later became known as Indian defenses. Strictly speaking, the Nimzo-Indian need not contain a fianchetto—and often does not as it is played today. Still there is always a possibility that a fianchetto will pop up; and, in Nimzovich's day, a deferred Queen-side fianchetto was generally pertinent against White patterns which that bold hypermodern encountered.

The Nimzo-Indian arises as follows:

1	P-Q4	N-KB3
2	P-QB4	P-K3
3	N-QB3	B-N5

With these three moves, a critical pattern has been set up, and the game has assumed its distinctive character.

Black's last move embraces a number of points:

1. The Bishop pins the Knight and neutralizes any effect the Knight may have on the center.

2. In some contingencies, the Bishop captures the Knight and leaves White with an awkward Pawn cluster.

3. A measure of aggression accrues to Black in the opening. Even a minimal initiative is generally denied the defender in nearly all openings.

4. No clear-cut system, leading to a plus for White, has yet been perfected.

As against these nebulous advantages, Black practically commits himself to parting with a Bishop for a Knight. While the difference between these two minor pieces is microscopic, it is nevertheless tangible.

4 Q-B2 . . . .

This move, too, embraces a number of ideas:

1. Should Black play *4* ... BxN, White is in position to recapture with his Queen and avoid doubled Pawns.

2. White clears the Queen file for occupation by his Queen Rook. This assures him a lead on the file, which may be of importance during the future course of the game.

3. Indirectly, White's Queen bears along the entire Bishop file. Often this action is pertinent to the later play.

Instead of the text move, there are any number of alternatives, each of which has been tried without leading to any pointed plus. Among them are *4* Q-N3, *4* N-B3, *4* P-QR3, and *4* P-K3. In some respects, these moves are sharper than others; they are, however, deficient, too. The text move and *4* P-K3 have been in vogue in master play since the thirties.

4 .... **P-Q4**

Immediately challenging for direct Pawn control of the center. Other lines begin with *4* ... P-B4, *4* ... N-B3, *4* ... O-O, *4* ... P-Q3, and *4* ... BxNch. Each of these alternatives leads to quite a different pattern.

After *4* ... P-B4, for example, the game may continue as follows: *5* PxP, N-B3; *6* N-B3, BxP; *7* B-N5, N-Q5; *8* NxN, BxN; *9* P-K3, Q-R4; *10* PxB, QxB; *11* B-Q3, O-O; *12* O-O, P-Q4; *13* P-B4. White's prospects are better. For one thing, Black's Queen is clumsily posted.

After *4* ... P-Q3, Black reserves the option of playing either ... P-Q4 or ... P-K4 later on. In each instance, however, with perfect play, White's chances are superior. For example, *4* ... P-Q3; *5* N-B3, QN-Q2; *6* B-Q2, O-O; *7* P-QR3, BxN;

8 BxB, Q-K2; 9 P-K3, P-K4; 10 B-K2, P-K5; 11 N-Q2, R-K1; 12 P-KN4, N-B1; 13 P-N5, with a plus for White. Black's King Pawn is under fire, White enjoys the advantage of the Bishop, and, to boot, there is a formidable King-side assault in the offing.

It does not follow from the foregoing examples that Black's play is perfect. Unquestionably, somewhere down the line a better plan may evolve.

5 PxP   . . . .

5 P-K3 defends White's Queen Bishop Pawn but shuts in White's Queen Bishop; whereas, after 5 N-B3, Black may make a serious effort to capture and hold the Queen Bishop Pawn by . . . PxP. That is the basis for the exchange.

5 . . . .   QxP

Centralizing the Queen, which is a good policy so long as the Queen cannot be molested. After 5 ... PxP, White may continue with N-B3, B-N5, and straightforward development. Then Black will have nothing better to do with his Queen Bishop than the retreat to K2, at the cost of losing a move, or exchanging it off for the Knight at the cost of giving up the minor exchange (a Bishop for a Knight).

6 N-B3   . . . .

White maintains his lead in development. 6 P-K3 is an alternative, though less appealing, since it shuts in White's Queen Bishop, even if only temporarily.

6 . . . .   P-B4

Black must demolish White's Pawn control of the center, while he is able. Any temporizing will result in an overwhelming position for the first player.

7 B-Q2   . . . .

Compelling Black to part with his Bishop for the Knight. If Black moves his Queen now, his development will become extremely laggard.

7 . . . .   BxN
8 BxB   . . . .

8 PxB is a sound reply, too. While the text move keeps the Queen Bishop file open, the Queen Bishop is transferred to another effective diagonal. Now, it points directly into the vicinity. of the Black monarch.

8 ....   **N-B3**

Developing apace. Not 8 ... N-K5; 9 PxP, and Black may not play 9 ... NxB because of 10 QxN, defending the extra Pawn.

9 **R-Q1!**   ....

Quickly to capitalize on the open Queen file.

9 ....   **O-O**

If now 9 ... QxRP; 10 PxP, O-O; 11 P-K4, White has a favorable position. After the text move, Black threatens to take off the Rook Pawn.

10 P-QR3 . . . .

Merely to defend the Pawn. There ought to be some way to defend the Pawn, without losing the move to advance it. Unfortunately, such is not the case.

10 . . . . **PxP**

Black simplifies by exchanging.

11 **NxP**	**NxN**
12 **RxN**	**Q-B3**
13 **P-K4**	**P-K4**
14 **R-B4**	. . . .

White is for choice, mainly because of his two Bishops. The edge is indeed minimal.

Conclusions and recommendations

Of all the defenses to the Queen Pawn Game, the Nimzo-Indian is currently the most popular. It is popular because Black has succeeded in getting more than his share of victories. This writer inclines to the belief that an opening which commits one side to parting with a Bishop for a Knight is theoretically unsound, and that in time, some way will be found to bolster White's play to grant him more than the usual initiative that is his due.

So far that way has not been found.

Chess Movie

THE TWO BISHOPS

THE WORLD TITLE is at stake in the following masterpiece
from the Alekhine–Euwe world championship bout, played in
Holland in 1937. Alekhine's Bishops rake the diagonals and
enmesh Euwe's poor Black monarch. The game begins with
1 P-Q4, N-KB3; *2* P-QB4, P-K3; *3* N-QB3, B-N5; *4* Q-B2, P-Q4.
Continue from Diagram 1.

1 Alekhine continues with
5 PxP, and there follows
5 ... QxP; *6* P-K3,
P-B4. A minimal initiative has
accrued to Black, but he is
committed to part with a
Bishop for a Knight to hold
his Queen in its dominant
position. The line is drawn
extremely fine, and the issue
is clear cut.

2 7 P-QR3 compels the
exchange. There follows
7 ... BxNch; *8* PxB.
Now White has a preponder-
ant Pawn center, while Black
has a temporary lead in the
development of his Knights.
8 ... QN-Q2 is Euwe's move.
How will Alekhine proceed to
utilize his forte—the powerful
Pawn center?

3 By playing *9 P-B3* and menacing *P-K4*, he undermines Black's security. This is a game of give and take. There follows *9 ... PxP; 10 BPxP, N-N3.* Momentarily, White's central demonstration is contained. It requires a bit of bolstering before Alekhine can push it through.

4 *11 N-K2* is Alekhine's move. The enemy Queen will be driven from its dominating post. Euwe continues to bring out his forces with *11 ... B-Q2.* There follows *12 N-B4, Q-Q3.* White's progress is slow but sure. Now Alekhine's aim is to assure an active role for his two Bishops.

5 *13 B-Q2* initiates their action. Black in turn develops his Rook with *13 ... R-QB1.* The Queen sidesteps the Rook with *14 Q-N2,* and Black attempts to penetrate or swap with *14 ... KN-Q4.* A few favorable exchanges will take all the zoom out of White's setup. Or so it seems, at least.

6 There follows *15 NxN, PxN.* Now White's center advance seems to be checked. The advance, *P-K4,* will leave the White Pawns in a tenuous state. But the Bishops must not yet be discounted. *16 B-N4* ties the Black King to the center of the board after *16 ... Q-K3.*

7   17 K-B2 safeguards the King Pawn and, incidentally, makes way for a Rook at King square. There follows *17 ... N-R5; 18 Q-Q2, P-QN3.* To maintain his Bishop at QN4, White continues with *19 B-R6,* and Black replies *19 ... R-QN1.* He now threatens to confine White's King Bishop.

8   Alekhine ignores Euwe's threat. The time has come to strike. *20 P-K4* opens the game, high, wide, and handsome. Euwe parries with *20 ... P-QN4.* White's Bishop *is* trapped. But wait! Alekhine has a counter: *21 Q-B4,* to which Euwe replies: *21 ... R-N3.* For the moment, all is well.

9   Now *22 PxP* opens the vital King file. White'll infiltrate with all his forces. Black plays *22 ... QxP,* and there follows *23 KR-K1ch, B-K3.* The King Bishop is still *en prise,* but tactical counterthreats have made it immune from capture, so far. What then is the next resource for White?

10   *24 QR-B1* is in fact the beginning of the end. The threat is R-B8ch. Black plays *23 ... P-B3,* and Alekhine continues with *25 R-B7.* The King will not escape. Euwe's last gasp is *25 ... K-Q1.* There follows *26 RxRP,* resigns. The power of the two Bishops has proved decisive.

10

The typical position in the Gruenfeld Defense

Gruenfeld Defense

THE WORLD of chess has witnessed a great search for new ways to cut down White's long-lasting initiative. Hypermodernism has introduced one whole and totally novel vista for the defense. The introduction of Alekhine's Defense, for example, taught that White may be lured into occupying the center—only *perhaps* to find that he has set up that center as a fixed and ready target for a Black counterstroke. The parallel idea, however, of an early sacrifice of the center against the Queen Pawn did not materialize so quickly. Not until 1922 did the Austrian master, Ernst Gruenfeld, evolve such a conscious and plausible system of defense.

The series of moves: *1* P-Q4, N-KB3; *2* P-QB4, P-KN3;

3 N-QB3, known as the King's Indian Defense, offered the opportunity. Gruenfeld veered from "the book" and audaciously essayed 3 ... P-Q4. His move enabled White to capture (4 PxP) and follow up immediately, after the recapture, with 5 P-K4, usurping all the dominant terrain in the middle of the board. Such a plan would have been frowned upon even less than half a century ago. And now—suddenly—it was good! What brought about the change of attitude? Was not the ceding of all the valuable, central squares tantamount to slow death?

The answers to these questions lie in the hypermodern approach. Black can afford to cede the center, if later he can make an appreciable dent there. That is the issue.

The Gruenfeld arises as follows:

1 P-Q4   N-KB3

From a purely theoretical standpoint, Black's move is good inasmuch as the Knight controls very important central squares. Since the Knight move is also a prelude to any number of Black defenses and, consequently, conceals the defender's specific plan, its "keep your opponent guessing" feature rates an additional plus.

2 P-QB4   . . . .

White builds a pattern that will mesh with any defense Black decides on. The advance of the Queen Bishop Pawn paves the way for White to continue quickly with N-QB3 and P-K4—obtaining a powerful lead in the center—unless Black proscribes this action.

2 . . . .   P-KN3

The King's Indian Defense. Black intends to fianchetto his King Bishop (B-N2), where it will bear down directly through the center of the board.

The fianchetto development has its good and bad points. While the Bishop at N2 strikes at the vital center, its effectiveness depends on what auxiliary support it will command from the rest of the Black forces. In other words, the Bishop at N2 will most likely bear down on a well-defended White Queen Pawn. Alone, the force of the Bishop will be meaningless. In conjunction with other forces bearing on the same sector, the fianchettoed Bishop may play an important role.

The Bishop at N2 exercises its influence on a commanding diagonal. On K2 or Q3 or some other square, the Bishop may be posted on a less valuable line, but its influence may go farther in other directions.

From a defensive point of view, also, the fianchetto is meritorious. The Bishop at N2 generally shields the position of its King at KN1, where it is apt to be. And the Pawn at KN3 limits the action of an enemy Bishop, bearing in the direction of Black's KR2.

On the other hand, Black's projected King Knight Pawn also is the source of possible weakness in that White may eventually institute a Pawn assault, which gains in momentum when, say, White's King Rook Pawn engages Black's King Knight Pawn.

All these considerations are involved in the simple fianchetto.

Instead of the text move, Black has a wide range of alternative replies. He may transpose into the Queen's Gambit by 2 ... P-K3 or 2 ... P-QB3, followed by ... P-Q4. Or he might even venture on the tricky Budapest Defense, 2 ... P-K4. This defense will be covered in a future chapter. Or he might try any number of other tenable, orthodox and unorthodox defenses.

3 **N-QB3** . . . .

The sharpest developing move, controlling the center and preparing to follow up with P-K4.

3 . . . . **P-Q4!**

The Gruenfeld, most important branch of the King's Indian Defense and, in fact, most popular.

At first sight, the text move appears to be a tactical violation of principle. For Black presents White with the opportunity to play 4 PxP, NxP; 5 P-K4, gaining full Pawn control of the central squares. There is, however, more to the move than the superficial appraisal discloses.

While Black cedes the center, he aims to open lines—files and diagonals—leading to White's center Pawns, which Black hopes will set up as a fixed target. The text move, for example, opens the Queen file so that later on, a Black Rook, posted on his Q1 square will press on White's Queen Pawn. With a Bishop at KN2, bearing on the same target, and most likely a Pawn at Black's QB4 square, White's Queen Pawn is apt to give. If that is the case, White's strong center becomes weak. And Black assumes the upper hand.

All this is based on "iffy" ideas. Nevertheless, the issue is drawn along these lines.

4 **PxP** . . . .

At this juncture, there is a great difference of opinion, even among the masters, as to what continuation offers White the best prospects. Of the alternative possibilities, the text move leads to a clearly defined pattern, wherein White is able to maintain the center.

4 Q-N3 held sway for a while and is still favored by some players. The point of this move is to avoid the exchange of Black's King Knight, which now only obstructs the diagonal intended for Black's King Bishop. In playing 4 Q-N3, however, White cannot build up a strong Pawn center quickly. Yet Black enjoys less counterplay. This line might go as follows: 4 Q-N3, P-B3; 5 N-B3, B-N2; 6 PxP, NxP; 7 P-K4, N-N3.

The straightforward 4 B-B4 is also a good alternative and leads to an infinitesimal plus in position for White. This line might go as follows: 4 B-B4, B-N2; 5 P-K3, O-O; 6 Q-N3, PxP; 7 KBxP, QN-Q2; 8 N-B3, N-N3; 9 B-K2, B-K3; 10 Q-B2, KN-Q4; 11 B-K5, R-B1; 12 NxN, QxN; 13 BxB, Q-R4ch; 14 Q-Q2, QxQch.

The moves Q-N3 and B-B4 can be interpolated by White by transposition in various lines of the Gruenfeld.

4 ....　　　NxP

Of course, Black must recapture; otherwise he is out a Pawn.

5 P-K4 　　　....

Here again, there are any number of patterns that might suit White's fancy: for instance, 5 P-KN3, followed by B-N2, or 5 P-K3 and 6 B-B4.

With the text move, White takes a stand in the center and feels that he will be able to meet Black's contemplated blows. In that event, White will come out on top.

5 ....   NxN

This and the next move are part and parcel of Black's grand plan. Should Black retreat his Knight to N3 or B3, he will not only have permitted White to build up a strong center, but he will also have lost time in development.

6 PxN   ....

Is the center weak or strong? At present the answer depends largely from which side the board is viewed!

6 ....   P-QB4!

The first blow at the enemy center. It involves the temporary sacrifice of a Pawn.

7 B-QB4   ....

To capture the Pawn is unwise. Thus, if 7 PxP, QxQch, and White forfeits the privilege of castling. Moreover, Black will sooner or later recover the Pawn by lining up against it on the open Queen Bishop file. When the Pawn is retrieved, White will then be left with a weaker Pawn structure.

7 P-Q5 is also an inferior alternative. In advancing the Pawn, White, of his own volition, breaks the solid front of his Pawn line and extends the scope of Black's King Bishop (when at KN2) to an attack on White's Queen Bishop Pawn.

The text move involves tactical considerations. White is looking ahead to the future. He wishes to support his Queen Pawn with his King Knight. But he has found, from previous experience, that the Knight is better posted on K2 than at B3. For at B3 it is subject to a pin by Black's Queen Bishop. Hence, in order not to cause interference in the ranks, White brings out his King Bishop and clears the path for a later N-K2. And at QB4, White's King Bishop bears down on the most vulnerable point in Black's camp—Black's KB2 square.

7 ....   **B-N2**

Developing as per plan. The Bishop strikes clearly throughout the center of the board, augmented in effect by Black's Pawn at his QB4.

8 **N-K2**   ....

Developing and defending the center. 8 N-B3 is less favorable, since Black can weaken White's center by 8 ... B-N5, pinning the Knight. Now 8 ... B-N5 is useless, as the Bishop can be driven by P-B3.

8 ....   **O-O**

Continuing his development and making ready for the pieces on the first rank to co-operate with each other. 8 ...

N-B3 is an alternative that can be met by 9 B-K3. By omitting to bring out his Knight to QB3 now, Black reserves the right to bring it out to Q2 later on.

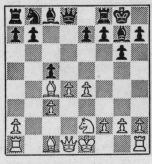

9 O-O   ....

White also completes his development and gains the co-operation of his forces on his first rank.

An interesting thought here is 9 P-Q5. While this move definitely breaches White's solid Pawn front, it offers the possibility of establishing a Pawn majority in the center (White's King Pawn and Queen Pawn versus Black's King Pawn), which then tends to restrict Black's movements. On the other hand, the weakness inherent in the advance might offset the gain. It is a moot question.

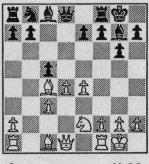

9 ....   N-Q2

After the more natural 9 … N-B3, there might follow
10 B-K3, Q-B2; 11 R-B1, R-Q1; 12 P-KR3, P-K4; 13 P-Q5. Then
White's passed Queen Pawn and Black's cramped position
would rule in White's favor.

The temporary obstruction of Black's Queen Bishop by
Black's Knight is of no real concern, since the Bishop will most
likely be developed on the flank at Black's QN2 square. From
that point of vantage, it also bears on White's center Pawns.

10 **B-KN5**   . . . .

Up to recently, 10 B-K3 was the usual move. The text move
is somewhat more precise, since the Bishop bears down on
Black's King Pawn and ties a Black man to its defense.

10 . . . .   **P-KR3**

To drive the Bishop. In doing so, however, Black weakens
his King-side Pawn structure to some extent.

11 **B-K3**   . . . .

Having provoked a slight weakness in Black's King-side
structure, the Bishop retreats. Its sights are now trained on
both wings.

11 . . . .   **Q-B2**

Clearing the path for ... R-Q1, to exert additional pressure on White's Queen Pawn. The move also threatens to win a piece by 12 ... PxP, simultaneously attacking two minor men.

12 R-B1 ....

So that if 12 ... PxP, 13 PxP, and White's Bishop is defended by the Rook.

12 .... P-R3

Since White's center holds firmly, Black must create a diversion on the wing. The text move is the prelude to the advance of Black's Queen-side Pawns. Black aims to establish a Pawn majority on that side.

13 Q-Q2 ....

Developing and attacking Black's King Rook Pawn, thanks to White's tenth move.

13 .... K-R2

White is for choice. Black has been unable to dent White's Pawn center.

White can now undertake action on the King-side by P-KB4-5, or he may inch in with N-B4-Q5.

Conclusions and recommendations

The Gruenfeld Defense, popular since its inception, has definitely added to the repertoire of those seeking to get away from the drab defenses to the Queen Pawn, which is the unhappy lot of the player of the Black men. From a theoretical point of view, it has had its ups and downs. Currently, opinion favors White, as Black is unable to make an appreciable dent in White's strong Pawn center.

♛ ♕ ⎍⎍⎍⎍⎍⎍⎍⎍⎍⎍⎍⎍⎍⎍⎍⎍ ♕ ♚

Chess Movie

THE PATHS OF GLORY

Struggle for supremacy invokes the gamut of all strategical and tactical concepts. Here hypermodernism tallies a telling success under the expert guidance of grand master, Dr. Feodor Bohatyrchuk (Black) against Savonov (White). The scene is Moscow, 1940. The game begins with *1* P-Q4, N-KB3; *2* P-QB4, P-KN3, *3* N-QB3, P-Q4 (and now continue from Diagram 1).

1 White adopts straightforward development: *4* B-B4. There follows *4* ... B-N2; *5* P-K3, O-O; *6* PxP, NxP. This is all a prelude to a predatory grab of a Pawn. In the interim, Black's development is promoted, and his men usurp the central squares. Is White's policy sound?

2 There follows 7 NxN, QxN; *8* BxP. White is now material plus. But Black assumes the initiative. Bohatyrchuk plays ·8 ... N-B3, continuing his development, and the game goes on with *9* N-K2, B-N5. (White hopes to bring his men out before Black can make an impression.)

110

3 First, however, White drives the advanced, enemy Bishop with *10* P-B3. This innocent rejoinder provokes the immediate assault. Black now counters with a piece sacrifice. *10 . . . QBxP* is the move! Can such things be and overcome us? Has Black lost track of values?

4 Of course, Savonov takes the Bishop. He plays *11* PxB, and Bohatyrchuk follows with *11 . . . QxBP;* attacking White's Rook. White moves his Rook: *12* R-KN1, and Black plays *12 . . . QxP.* Now he has two Pawns and a creditable onslaught for the piece. The scales are delicately balanced.

5 Because his King is somewhat exposed, White attempts to consolidate. The game continues *13* B-B4, Q-K5; *14* B-N2, Q-B4; *15* Q-Q2. Now White readies for Queen-side castling, when all will be well. Then the extra man will more than make up for the absence of the Pawns—White hopes.

6 There is, however, no rest for the wicked. *15 . . .* P-K4 places new obstacles in White's path and at the same time opens new lines. White plays *16* BxN, and there follows *16* KPxB; *17* B B3, KR-K1. (Black has fouled up White's plan. If White now castles, *. . .* RxN! is the sockdolager.)

7 White accommodates himself to the new conditions. He plays *18* K-B2, and Black penetrates with *18 ... R-K6*. White feints a counterdemonstration with *19* R-N4, which Black ignores with *19 ...* QR-K1. There follows *20* QR-KN1, B-R3. White still has his piece, but not his peace!

8 White stalls with *21* R-R4, and Black routs the defense with *21 ...* R-Q6. The White lady flees with *22* Q-N4, and Black tears through with *22 ...* RxBch. Black has scored the first check and now there is no letup. The mating net is set. Only a few loopholes must be closed.

9 Savonov feebly gestures a retreat with *23* K-K1. This is tantamount to an admission of defeat. And now comes the incisive *23 ...* RxNch, which must be respected. And it is. White plays *24* KxR, and Black follows relentlessly with *24 ...* Q-Q6ch. The rest should be silence.

10 *25* K-K1 is the move. Black follows up with *25 ...* R-K6ch. All the avenues of escape lead to mate. The White monarch is cornered. Savonov plays *26* K-B2, and Bohatyrchuk follows with *26 ...* Q-K7 mate. Hypermodernism has wound up in a crowning blaze of glory.

11

The typical position in the Budapest

Budapest Defense

Bᴇ ɪᴛ ɢᴏᴏᴅ, bad, or indifferent, every debut embraces a strong point. There is hardly an opening in Caissa's repertoire —whether the Corkscrew or the Ghulim Kassim—which does not rate a potent wallop. Intensify the forte and subdue the weakness is the governing strategy of inferior openings.

So it is with the Budapest, a precarious defense. On his second move, Black sacrifices a whole Pawn! The magnitude of this gesture can be appraised in the light of comparison. When White gives up a Pawn in the opening, its soundness rests, so to speak, on a hair. When Black does so with a move behind, the odds are overwhelmingly against its validity. Yet, despite this exceedingly slim factor of safety, many a defender plays the Budapest. Why?

To begin with, there is always the psychological reason. A player taken by surprise and not conversant with the theoretical details of an idea is apt to go wrong. White may go wrong. And then there is the inherent, although insignificant, forte of the defense, which grows to great proportions, if not properly conquered. Add these two factors together, and there is reason enough for the adventuresome chess-player to play any opening.

The Budapest is one of the later-day openings. It made its advent about 1915, and its popularity rose for quite a while. It has been used especially by American masters: Kevitz, Simonson, and Bisguier, for example. Thorough analysis, however, has revealed its weak points, and today it crops up only occasionally in the tournament arena.

The Budapest arises as follows:

	1	P-Q4	N-KB3
	2	P-QB4	....

White's first two moves are characteristic of the Queen Pawn Game. Their purpose is to maintain pressure on the central squares, K5 and Q5.

2 .... P-K4!?

Black's move is a most unusual Pawn sacrifice. At first sight, it appears pointless; it neither promotes development nor opens lines. Despite these apparent drawbacks, it is not completely without merit. White is beset at once with a problem of refutation.

3 PxP   ....

Other moves, such as 3 N-KB3 or 3 P-K3, lead to tenable variations, but with no perceptible advantage. On the contrary, the declination of the gambit can be considered as a moral victory for the defender, inasmuch as he has steered the play into a line not contemplated by White. General principles, moreover, dictate that a Pawn should be captured when offered, unless its acceptance interferes with a necessary defense or greater gain in some other direction.

The reason for Black's Pawn sacrifice, as yet, is not clear; but it will become evident as the game progresses.

3 ....   N-N5

The text move is the one generally employed by Black. It aims to recover the Pawn or to provoke fundamental weaknesses in White's Pawn structure.

An alternative, recently popularized but still found wanting is 3 ... N-K5, known as the Fajarowicz Variation. The line may run as follows: 3 ... N-K5; 4 Q-B2, P-Q4; 5 PxP e.p., B-B4; 6 N-QB3!, NxQP; 7 P-K4, NxKP (otherwise Black has nothing for the Pawn minus); 8 B-Q3, NxP; 9 BxB, NxR; 10 N-B3, B-B4; 11 N-K4, Q-K2; 12 B-N5 with a plus for White. The above is from the match game, Kottnauer–Martin, Czecho-

Slovakia—France, 1946. The game continued *12* ... P-KB3; *13* O-O-O!, N-R3; *14* R-Q7 with an overwhelming position. If, in this line, *12* ... B-N5ch; *13* K-K2, P-KB3; *14* B-K3, White still maintains the lead.

4 B-B4 . . . .

This is one of a number of alternative possibilities. The text move is the beginning of a concerted effort to maintain the extra Pawn in a positional way.

If White favors an attack, he may venture upon the following line: *4* P-K4, NxKP; *5* P-B4, N-N3; *6* N-KB3, N-B3; *7* P-QR3 (to drive Black's Bishop from Black's QB4, when it goes there), P-QR4; *8* B-K3, P-QN3; *9* N-B3, B-B4. Despite White's superior command of the central terrain, his advantage is questionable because his Pawns are advanced and have a weak quality about them. It may well be, in fact, that Black's prospects are better.

The sequence of the text move is of paramount importance. If White plays *4* N-KB3, for example, his extra Pawn is doomed, thus: *4* ... B-B4; *5* P-K3, N-QB3; followed by ... Q-K2.

4 . . . . **N-QB3**

Black piles up on the extra Pawn with a view to recovering it.

5 N-KB3 . . . .

White protects the Pawn and develops at the same time.

5 ....   **B-N5ch**

This check is one of the tactical moves in the defense. It limits White's replies, which will be examined later.

Another way is 5 ... P-B3; 6 PxP, QxP; 7 Q-Q2, B-N5; 8 N-B3, BxN; 9 PxB, P-Q3; 10 P-K3, P-QN3; 11 B-K2, B-N2; 12 O-O, N-K2; 13 N-Q4, N-K4; 14 B-N3, O-O-O; 15 P-B4, with a plus for White. White's King is comparatively safe and Black's King can be smoked out sooner or later. Note particularly that White has an extra center Pawn, which will require consideration. This line is from the match game, Eliskases–Bogolyubov, 1939.

6 **N-B3**   ....

6 QN-Q2 leaves White with a trifling positional advantage, thus: *6* ... Q-K2; *7* P-QR3, KNxKP (threatening *8* ... N-Q6 mate!); *8* NxN, NxN; *9* P-K3, BxNch; *10* QxB, P-Q3; *11* O-O.

White enjoys the advantage of the two Bishops. This, however, may be insufficient for a decision.

6 ....   **Q-K2**

Still piling onto the Pawn.

7 **Q-Q5**   ....

Still defending.

7 ....   **BxNch**

The point. White's Queen-side Pawn structure is left in shambles, and Black reckons this as compensation for his Pawn minus. That this is sufficient, however, is a moot question.

8 **PxB**   **Q-R6**

An immediate attempt to exploit the weak Pawns.

9 **R-B1**   ....

Practically forced. But good enough. If 9 Q-Q2, Q-B4 recovers the Pawn by virtue of the triple attack on various assorted Pawns.

9 . . . .   **P-B3**

Black hardly has time to pick off the White Rook Pawn, since White threatens to drive the King Knight by P-KR3 to an awkward post.

With the text move, Black resigns himself to the permanent loss of the Pawn, but hopes that his better Pawn position will serve as compensation.

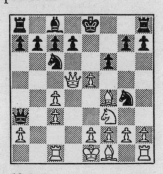

10 PxP   . . . .

White must capture. Otherwise Black recovers the Pawn and maintains the superior position. And not *10* P-K6, PxP; *11* Q-R5ch, P-N3; *12* QxN, P-K4; with a plus for Black.

10 . . . .   **NxP/3**

After which all of Black's men are fairly well disposed. But the Pawn minus still lurks in the background.

11 **Q-Q2**   **P-Q3**

Black guards the unprotected Queen Bishop Pawn and prepares the development of the Queen-side men.

12 **N-Q4**   . . . .

Centralizing the Knight, which is more or less immune, since Black cannot afford to capture and straighten out White's Pawns.

12 .... **O-O**

Continuing the natural development.

13 **P-B3** ....

Preparing for P-K4 and the annexation of the center, while, at the same time, avoiding a pitfall: *13* P-K3??, NxN; *14* BPxN, N-K5; *15* Q-B2, Q-R4ch; *16* K-K2, RxB; *17* PxR, B-B4; *18* Q-N2, R-K1; with a powerful attack—Rubinstein–Vidmar, Berlin, 1918.

White is for choice. His extra Pawn is the deciding factor.

Conclusions and recommendations

Every theoretical and practical conclusion on the Budapest grants White a decided advantage. This writer, nevertheless, harbors a feeling that somehow the Budapest will eventually be vindicated. In any case, those who enjoy unbalanced positions and flights of fancy will find the Budapest a happy medium.

Chess Movie

WHO KILLED COCK ROBIN?

Victory in a chess game indicates one or more blunders on the part of the vanquished. A piece *en prise,* an inadvertent, overlooked mate, something awry—all spell disaster. In the 1936 U.S. Championship, Hanauer (White) follows the prescribed technique and loses to Horowitz. Where did he err? The game begins: *1* P-Q4, N-KB3; *2* P-QB4, P-K4; *3* PxP, N-N5; *4* N-KB3, B-B4; *5* P-K3, N-QB3 (see first diagram).

1 White follows a system recommended by Alekhine. His long-term idea is to dominate his Q5 square. There follows: *6* P-QR3, P-QR4; *7* N-B3, KNxP/4; *8* B-K2, O-O. Black has succeeded in restraining White's aspirations to expand on the Queen-side. White's position and Black's are both structurally sound.

2 The game continues with *9* O-O, P-Q3; *10* P-QN3, readying for the development of the Queen Bishops. There follows: *10* ... NxNch; *11* BxN, N-K4. Since Black's Bishops are pointed in the general direction of the enemy King, Black plans to launch an incursion on that wing. What is his method?

121

3 Out comes White's Queen Bishop with *12 B-N2*, and Black replies *12 ... Q-R5*. One by one, his forces approach the target. White rejoins *13 N-Q5*, and Black drives the Knight with *13 ... P-QB3*. His Queen Pawn becomes backward, but he gains time in order to bring up reinforcements.

4 There follows: *14 N-B3, B-B4; 15 B-K2, QR-K1*. Somehow, White has let his initiative slip. The game continues: *16 Q-Q2, R-K3*. Oddly enough, White is now doomed. In only a move or two, all the heavy artillery will be bearing on White's King. And what is White to do about it?

5 Hastily White musters a defense. *17 N-Q1* is the move. There follows: *17 ... R-R3*, and White is embarrassed. The Rook Pawn is a "goner." White cuts down the potential onslaught by *18 BxN*, and then Black recaptures with *18 ... PxB*. The backward Pawn is gone; but the attack remains.

6 *19 P-R3* is White's move. Black pursues his course with *19 ... QBxP*. The Bishop is immune from capture on account of the exposed position of White's King. The multifarious threats leave White without resource. He counters with *20 P-N3*, and Black replies with *20 ... Q-K5* with grim effect.

7 Mate is threatened, and White can safely resign. But who gives up the ghost when he is so materially rich. Feebly, White continues with 21 P-B3, and Black follows up with 21 ... Q-N3. Now again, mate is in the offing. White defends with 22 K-B2, and Black captures with 22 ... BxR.

8 White recaptures with 23 BxB, and Black plays 23 ... P-K5. The hardest game to win is a won game; so Black continues sharply. There follows: 24 P-B4, Q-N5. Black infiltrates the punctured position. The threat now extant at KB3 requires prompt attention, likewise that at his KR2.

9 There follows: 25 B-N2, R-N3. Now the King Knight Pawn falls, and with it also White's whole King-side structure. White plays 26 K-B1, and Black captures: 26 ... QxNP. White offers a friendly exchange of Queens, with 27 Q-KB2. And, after all, why should Black refuse? He plays 27 ... QxQch.

10 White, of course, recaptures. 28 KxQ is his move. Black follows with 28 ... P-B4, and then the sequel is 29 R-R2, R-Q3; 30 N-B3, R-Q6. After that, White faces a current deficit of an exchange and two Pawns—with yet another Pawn going. White has had enough. White resigns.

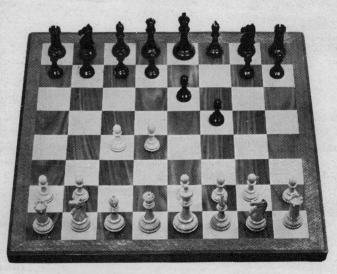

The typical position in the Dutch Defense

Dutch Defense

Orthodox defenses to the Queen's Pawn Game encounter a gantlet of trying problems. Black's Queen Bishop, for example, is the perennial offender in most usual variations. Its development leaves the Queen Knight Pawn unguarded, and this, in turn, is subject to peremptory exploitation. Symmetrical lines give White a lasting initiative; other lines, emanating from these defenses, grant White spacious domain and sound structures, while Black is cramped and often crippled. Orthodox defenses leave much to be desired.

Irregular and independent defenses also suffer from certain drawbacks. In short, Black's lot is not a happy one.

With the points to be solved in proper focus, however, the pursuit has been for a defense which yields a measure of *Lebensraum* and counterplay, without risking too many structural defects. Such is the Dutch Defense.

After the moves, *1* P-Q4, P-K3; *2* P-QB4, Black essays *2 . . .* P-KB4. Immediately, the pattern of the position is unbalanced. White presses on his Q5, while Black bears down on his K5. Point and counterpoint. By the very nature of his defense, Black enjoys a fighting formation. Add to this the desirability of determining the opening and that of employing a not too well-analyzed sequence of moves, and there is reason enough to justify the Dutch.

The Dutch, sometimes called the Hollandish Defense, dates from 1775, when it was first noted in *Traité des Amateurs*. In 1779, it was elaborated upon in Stein's *Nouvel Essai sur les Échecs*. Today, it is included in the repertoire of leading masters, with World Champion Botvinnik among its stalwart disciples.

The Dutch arises as follows:

1 **P-Q4**   **P-K3**

The original Hollandish Defense arose after *1* P-Q4, P-KB4. While the interpolation, *1 . . .* P-K3, leaves Black open to a French Defense*, it is a "risk" that he must assume. Otherwise,

* After *2* P-K4.

he must chance the perilous Staunton Gambit: *1* P-Q4, P-KB4; *2* P-K4!, in which each side treads on thin ice. While it is possible that the gambit may be contained, practical odds favor the aggressor. A model game, Denker–Dake, Syracuse, 1934, runs as follows: *2* ... PxP; *3* P-KB3, P-K3; *4* N-Q2, PxP; *5* KNxP, N-KB3; *6* B-Q3, P-B4; *7* O-O, PxP; *8* N-N5, P-Q4; *9* NxRP, with a powerful attack.

2 P-QB4   P-KB4
(See photo)

The Dutch Defense as it is generally played today. From the point of view of dominating the central squares, the formation favors White. Observe that his Pawns strike at K5, Q5, QB5, and QN5—squares in or near the center—while Black's Pawns strike at K5, KN5, and Q4. Those squares of immediate moment, however, are White's Q5 and Black's K5. Though important for the long term, the other squares are of subsidiary significance.

One other consideration is worthy of note. The advance of Black's King Bishop Pawn—a Pawn in Black's King's sector—has a tendency to weaken the monarch's position. It is for this reason, in fact, that the Staunton Gambit (mentioned previously) is tenable.

The unbalanced nature of the text position indicates a fighting game, with threats and counterthreats in different fields.

3 P-KN3   . . . .

Preparatory to the fianchetto of the King Bishop, which is a direct challenge to Black's control of his K5 square.

Alternate lines grant White equally good prospects. Even the simple development of each Knight at B3, followed by B-KB4, P-K3 and B-Q3 is fair enough. The text line is in favor today, possibly because it is meeting with success.

3 . . . .   N-KB3

Developing apace and bearing down on K5.

4 B-N2 ....

As per plan.

4 .... **B-K2**

4 ... B-N5ch has been tried and found wanting. White can play 5 B-Q2 or 5 N-Q2, in each case with the better prospects. The latter may be preferred since the Bishop at N5 is practically committed to the exchange of Bishop for Knight—a welcome exchange for White.

5 N-KB3 ....

This move, as is well known, commands vital center squares. Alternatives are 5 N-Q2 and 5 N-KR3. The former practically forces Black to adopt the Stonewall formation with 5 ... P-Q4, since it threatens 6 P-K4, opening lines that will eventually lead to the Black King. True enough, the Stonewall is playable. With Black's laggard development, however, he must be wary of creating holes in his position. (Note the hole at Black's K4 square, after the move ... P-Q4.) The maneuver 5 N-KR3-B4 has also been tried with fair success.

It is difficult to say which of the alternatives grants White the best prospects. White stands well in each line.

5 .... **O-O**

Before defining his plan for bringing out the rest of his forces, Black gets his King into comparative safety.

6 O-O   ....

White follows suit. White still controls the greater portion of the central squares and maintains the minimal initiative vested in him with the first move.

6 .... **P-Q4**

The text is the Stonewall formation. Black's Pawns are posted as a powerful barrier against enemy incursion. To boot, Black fortifies his hold on the square K5. Despite these salient features, the move has inherent defects. For one thing, White now gains unchallenged command of his K5 square. Again, Black's position is backward and with a serious hole at his K4 square. Nevertheless, it is difficult for White to exploit the defects, and if he is slightly remiss, Black can work up a creditable onslaught against the White King by transferring his men to that side of the board.

The alternative line is 6 ... P-Q3. The game might then pursue the following course: *7* N-B3, Q-K1; *8* R-K1, Q-R4; *9* P-K4, PxP; *10* NxP, NxN; *11* RxN, N-B3; *12* B-B4, B-B3; *13* P-KR4, P-KR3; *14* R-B1, P-R3; *15* P-B5 with a plus for White. Black's development is deficient and his backward King Pawn is a chronic weakness.

7 P-N3   ....

To transfer the Queen Bishop to an effective diagonal on the left wing.

7 ....   **P-B3**

Part and parcel of the Stonewall formation. Black's plan is to build an invulnerable Pawn barrier and then proceed slowly with his men to the King-side. The idea is good, if it works!

8 **N-K5**   ....

White, however, is not without resource. One thing is almost certain: if, in a given position, one side has an advantage, correct play can do no worse than maintain an even balance. White's advantage in the present setup is marked. He controls the greater portion of the center; his hold on K5 cannot be challenged by an adverse Pawn and he has considerable more *Lebensraum*. A Black Knight at its K5 can be driven by a White Pawn. Consequently, at best, Black may achieve only equality.

White's Knight on K5 now dominates the center in all directions.

8 ....   **QN-Q2**

Merely to bring out the men and not necessarily to swap Knights.

9 N-Q3   . . . .

White can afford to leave his Knight on K5. For, if Black exchanges, White's Pawn on K5 exerts a cramping effect on Black's development. In restrained positions, however, every exchange simplifies and, to a small degree, lessens the problem of the defender. That is why White retreats. His Knight on Q3 makes difficult any liberating attempt on Black's part.

9 . . . .   Q-K1

To swing the Queen over to the King-side, most likely to KR4.

10 P-B3!   . . . .

More than anything else, this move shows up the weakness of Black's position. Now Black cannot play . . . N-K5. Moreover, White plans an eventual P-K4. Thus, Black's hold on his K5 square has practically vanished.

	10	**P-QN3**

To free the Queen Bishop for action via the Queen-side.

	11 **B-N2**	**B-N2**

Development goes on apace.

	12 **N-Q2**	...

Readying for P-K4.

	12	**P-B4!**

This break is highly necessary. Otherwise, after P-K4-5, Black will remain permanently cramped.

	13 **P-K3**	....

Thus, Black has contained White's threat of P-K4 in the nick of time.

	13	**R-B1**

From here on, Black's position is somewhat freer than before. White's advantage now is the weakness of Black's King Pawn, plus the fact that he can occupy his K5 at some later time, unchallenged by an enemy Pawn.

White is for choice.

Conclusions and recommendations

The Dutch Defense falls in the category of the lesser analyzed openings and, as such, grants a player conversant with its details a creditable opportunity to play for a win with the Black men. Theoretically, White's structure is the sounder. Not so much so, however, as to prove fatal.

Chess Movie

THERE OUGHTA BE A LAW

W<small>HEN</small> K<small>NIGHTS</small> are developed on the wing and Bishops are swapped for Knights with impunity, sacrosanct tenets are violated. The culprit ought to be punished. Instead, here he is rewarded! Dutch master, S. Landau (White) defeats the inimitable Tartakover in the following game at Rotterdam, 1931. The game begins with *1* P-Q4, P-K3; *2* P-QB4, P-KB4; *3* P-KN3, N-KB3; *4* B-N2, reaching Diagram 1.

1 Tartakover continues with the old-fashioned check—*4* ... B-N5ch. There follows *5* B-Q2, Q-K2. Now Landau apparently violates general principles with *6* N-KR3, and the learned Doctor plays *6* ... N-K5. For the present, it appears that Black is making progress.

2 Oddly enough, White again violates principles: he plays *7* BxN. To violate *a principle*, we learn, is bad. To violate *principles* possibly is another story. Anyway, the game continues *7* ... PxB; *8* O-O, BxB; *9* NxB, P-Q4. Clearly, White leads in development—all of a sudden.

3 The secret is out. White plays *10* N-B4, and the Knight is no longer on a limb; it is well centralized. Black plays *10* ... P-QB3, and White increases the pressure with *11* Q-N3. After *11* ... O-O, White breaks with *12* P-B3! There follows *12* ... KPxP; *13* RxP. White will double Rooks.

4 White's threat to double Rooks on the King Bishop file throws a scare into Tartakover. He plays for simplification. *13* ... P-KN4 is the move. There follows *14* N-N2, RxR; *15* QxR, N-Q2. The position is somewhat simplified; but Black's King Knight Pawn is a pronounced weakness.

5 Landau plays *16* R-KB1, and Tartakover attends to his Queenside with *16* ... P-N3. Soon, his Bishop will come out on the flank. There follows *17* Q-K3, B-R3; *18* PxP, BPxP. Thus far, Black has parried the obvious threats. Now his defense is much more difficult. Notably because of his weak Pawns.

6 White trains his guns on the target. *19* N-B3 is the move. Black follows with *19* ... P-N5, and White penetrates with *20* N-N5. Among other threats, the King Pawn is attacked. Black defends with *20* ... N-B1. *21* R-B7 signals the beginning of the final assault. *21* ... Q-Q3 follows.

7 Can Black survive the head-on clash? The answer is no! White plays 22 Q-B2 (threatening Q-B6). Black perforce rejoins with 22 ... P-K4. And White tastes first blood with 23 RxKRP. Since the Rook is immune from capture, Black responds 23 ... Q-N3, for defense and counterplay.

8 At first sight, it appears that White was too impetuous. For now, two pieces are *en prise*. But White was prepared. 24 N-R4! is the proper continuation, and Black is embarrassed. He makes the most of the worst: 24 ... NxR; 25 NxQ, NxN. A powerful Queen for two lesser pieces is his (forced) deal.

9 It is White's move—fortunately. What a difference one puny move makes! Black could win with ... N-R6ch, but White continues with 26 Q-B6, and Black is moving out of sheer impetus. Now comes the spite check. 26 ... N-R6ch is the move. Black can safely resign; but will he?

10 Landau replies 27 K-N2, and Tartakover hangs on by the skin of his bridgework with 27 ... R-K1. Now follows 28 NxP, with a plethora of threats. Q-N6ch, Q-B7ch, NxP, etc., are menacing. White can win a Rook, a Knight or a King. Black resigns. Naturally.

Theoretically Important Games

Game 1: CENTER GAME
(Scheveningen, 1913)

	J. MIESES *White*			A. ALEKHINE *Black*
1	P-K4	P-K4	5	N-QB3	B-K2
2	P-Q4	PxP	6	B-Q2	O-O
3	QxP	N-QB3	7	O-O-O	P-Q4!
4	Q-K3	N-B3	8	PxP	NxP

A typical situation in this opening: White's Queen will either be useless or a target during the remaining play.

9	Q-N3	B-R5!	10	Q-B3	B-K3
			11	B-K3	NxN!

In return for the Queen Black gets Rook, Knight, and Pawn —plus a lasting initiative based on the White Queen's inactivity!

12 RxQ	NxPch	17 R-QB1	P-KN3
13 K-N1	QRxR	18 P-N4	B-K5
14 B-K2	N/R7-N5	19 Q-R3	B-B3
15 N-R3	KR-K1!	20 B-B3	BxB
16 N-B4	B-B4	21 QxB	N-K4
		22 Q-K2	P-B4!

This Pawn will play an important role in the final attack. White's Queen is a spectator to the end.

23 R-N1	P-B5	25 NxN	RxN
24 P-R4	N-Q4	26 P-B4	N-Q6!

The brilliant Knight move exploits a new weakness in White's camp, as 27 PxN, RxP; 28 R-N3, B-Q5 does not look inviting to him.

27 Q-B3	R-QN4!	31 P-N5	R/B1-B7!
28 PxN	RxPch	32 K-K1	R-N8ch
29 K-B1	PxP	33 Q-Q1	B-B6ch
30 K-Q1	R-QB1!		Resigns

A brilliant attack by Black (though 33 ... R-K7ch is more exact). The White Queen has been useless from beginning to end.

Game 2: CENTER GAME
(Postal Game, 1932–33)

M. VON FEILITSCH
White

P. KERES
Black

	White		Black
1	P-K4	P-K4	
2	P-Q4	PxP	
3	QxP	N-QB3	
4	Q-K3	N-B3	
5	N-QB3	B-N5	
6	B-Q2	O-O	

7	O-O-O	R-K1
8	B-QB4	P-Q3
9	P-B3	N-QR4!
10	B-Q3	P-Q4
11	Q-N5	P-KR3!
12	Q-R4	P-Q5

Black has freed himself and soon begins a withering attack. As in the previous game, White's Queen will be little more than an innocent bystander.

13	QN-K2	.BxBch
14	RxB	P-B4

15	P-QB4	B-K3
16	P-QN3	P-QN4!

So that if *17* PxP, BxP!; *18* PxB, NxPch; *19* K-B2, NxR; *20* KxN, NxPch!; winning the Queen!

17	N-B4	PxP
18	NxB	RxN
19	PxP	R-N1
20	N-K2	Q-N3!

21	K-Q1	Q-N5
22	Q-N3	N-Q2!
23	R-B2	Q-R6!
24	P-B4	R-KN3!
25	Q-B3	RxP!

Black winds up his brilliant attack with a few convincing strokes.

26 P-K5	R-QN8ch!	29 QxN	PxQ
27 R-B1	NxBP!!	30 B-B4	Q-R5ch!
28 RxR	N-K6ch	Resigns	

White must lose another piece. Whereas Black's Queen was in the thick of the fight, the White Queen played the inglorious role that is typical of this opening.

Game 3: DANISH GAMBIT
(Baden, 1914)

G. NYHOLM *White*		R. RETI *Black*	
1 P-K4	P-K4	5 BxP	PxP
2 P-Q4	PxP	6 QBxP	N-KB3
3 P-QB3	PxP	7 N-KB3	B-N5ch!
4 B-QB4	P-Q4	8 K-B1	....

A sad decision, but if 8 N-B3, NxB; 9 PxN, Q-K2ch; and White can hardly interpose 10 Q-K2, allowing the exchange of Queens when a Pawn down. It is already clear that White has nothing to show for his minus Pawn.

8	O-O!	9 Q-N3	N-B3!

Sprightly play. He is not afraid of 10 BxN, PxB; 11 QxB? because of 11 ... R-N1!!; 12 Q-B3, RxB!; 13 QxR??, Q-Q8ch; 14 N-K1, B-R3ch; and mate follows.

10 N-B3	Q-K2!	16 B-K2	B-K3
11 P-QR3	B-Q3!	17 Q-B2	Q-B4!
12 R-K1	N-K4	18 R-B1	KR-Q1
13 NxN	BxN	19 P-N3	P-QR4
14 B-B4	P-B3!	20 Q-N1	R-Q7!
15 P-KR4	P-QN4	21 N-Q5	RxQB!

A nice finish. The idea is that after 22 NxNch, PxN; 23 QxR, BxQ; 24 RxQ, BxP; 25 RxBP, P-N5; the passed Pawns walk in.

22 QxR	QxN!	24 R-B2	BxQP
23 PxQ	BxQ	Resigns	

Game 4: DANISH GAMBIT
(Postal Game, 1948)

R. E. HODURSKI White		G. M. CROWLEY Black	
1 P-K4	P-K4	6 BxQP	N-KB3
2 P-Q4	PxP	7 BxPch!	KxB
3 P-QB3	PxP	8 QxQ	B-N5ch
4 B-QB4	PxP	9 Q-Q2	BxQch
5 BxP	P-Q4	10 NxQ	P-B4

A definite improvement on White's play in the previous game. For many years it was thought that this position favors

Black—because of his Queen-side majority of Pawns. Actually, as we shall see, White has the better of it because of his superior development and because his King Pawn and King Bishop Pawn can advance menacingly if given a chance.

| 11 | KN-B3 | B-K3 | | 13 | NxB | KxN |
| 12 | N-N5ch | K-K2 | | 14 | P-B4 | P-QN4? |

Black does not realize the gravity of the situation. Development with *14 . . . N-B3* was his best chance. From this point on, White steadily increases his command of the board until he has a strangle hold.

15	P-B5ch	K-B2		21	R-Q1ch	K-B1
16	P-K5	N-K1		22	R-Q7	R-N1
17	P-K6ch	K-K2		23	P-N4	P-R3
18	N-K4	N-R3		24	N-Q6ch	NxN
19	O-O-O	R-Q1		25	RxN	N-N1
20	RxR	KxR		26	B-K5!	P-B5
				27	P-K7!	Resigns

A tragicomic situation. White threatens to win a piece with *28 R-Q8ch!*

Black cannot save himself with *27 . . . N-Q2;* for then *28 R-B6ch, K-N2; 29 R-B7ch* wins the miserable Knight.

Game 5: KING'S GAMBIT
(Stuttgart, 1939)

G. KIENINGER		E. ELISKASES	
White		*Black*	
1 P-K4	P-K4	3 N-KB3	N-KB3
2 P-KB4	PxP	4 N-B3	. . . .

As pointed out on page 33, 4 P-K5 is the move. However, this game is quoted in all the standard opening books, and as the full score is extremely hard to come by, it is given here.

4	P-Q4	9 K-B2	B-KB4
5 PxP	NxP	10 P-B5	N-B3!
6 NxN	QxN	11 B-N5	Q-Q4!
7 P-Q4	B-K2	12 BxP	O-O-O
8 P-B4	Q-K5ch	13 B-K3	B-B3!
		14 Q-R4	B-K5!

Ruthlessly following up his plan of piling up on the weakened Queen Pawn, Black envisages the sacrifice of a whole Rook.

Black has this astonishing line up his sleeve: *15* BxN, QxB; *16* QxP, BxN; *17* PxB, BxP; *18* BxB, RxB; *19* Q-R8ch, K-Q2; *20* QxR, QxQBP!; and White is lost!

15	BxN	QxB
16	QxQ	BxQ
17	QR-Q1	KR-K1

18	KR-K1	BxN!
19	KxB	BxP!
20	BxB	RxR
21	RxR	RxB

Black has won the weak Pawn as planned, but White has counterplay, with resulting drawing chances.

22	R-K7!	R-Q2
23	R-K8ch	R-Q1
24	R-K7	R-B1
25	P-QN4	P-QR3
26	P-QR4	K-Q1
27	R-K4	K-Q2
28	P-N5	PxP
29	PxP	R-QR1

30	R-Q4ch	K-K3
31	R-K4ch	K-B3
32	R-Q4	R-R6ch
33	K-K4	R-QB6
34	K-Q5	P-N4?!
35	R-Q2	P-N3?!
36	PxP	PxP
37	K-Q6!	R-B4
38	R-Q5!	....

Curiously enough, Black cannot win the ending. His Queen Knight Pawn is too weak.

38	....	R-B7
39	P-N4	RxP
40	K-B6	P-R4
41	PxP	RxP
42	KxP	K-K3

43	K-B6	P-B4
44	P-N6	R-R1
45	P-N7	P-N5
46	R-Q6ch	K-K4
47	K-B7	P-N6

If now 48 P-N8/Q??, White loses!

48	R-Q8!	R-R2ch
49	R-Q7	R-R1

50	R-Q8	R-R2ch
51	R-Q7	Drawn

A fascinating game.

Game 6: KING'S GAMBIT
(Southsea, 1951)

P. RAVN
White

A. O'KELLY DE GALWAY
Black

1	P-K4	P-K4		6	O-O	N-QB3
2	P-KB4	PxP		7	P-Q4	P-Q4
3	N-KB3	B-K2		8	PxP e.p.	BxP
4	B-B4	N-KB3		9	R-K1ch	N-K2
5	P-K5	N-N5		10	P-KR3	N-KB3

Black has a good development, and he can hold on to the gambit Pawn without compromising his position with ... P-KN4. He has already refuted the gambit.

11	N-B3	O-O		15	P-B4	Q-B3
12	N-QN5	N-N3		16	P-QN4	N-N6
13	NxB	PxN!		17	B-N2	B-B4
14	B-Q3	N-R4		18	P-QR4	KR-K1

Black steadily improves his position.

19	Q-Q2	BxB		21	Q-N3	N/N3-R5!
20	QxB	N-B4		22	NxN	NxN
				23	Q-B2	P-B6!

Beginning the final phase.

24 P-Q5	Q-N4		28 B-B1	Q-B3
25 P-N4	P-KR4		29 R-R3	PxP
26 Q-B1	RxRch		30 K-R2	P-B7
27 QxR	PxP		31 Q-B1	Q-K4ch
			Resigns	

The coming ... Q-K8 will be crushing.

Game 7: KING'S GAMBIT DECLINED
(Maehrisch–Ostrau, 1923)

A. RUBINSTEIN *White*		K. HROMADKA *Black*	
1 P-K4	P-K4	7 P-KR3	BxN
2 P-KB4	B-B4	8 QxB	N-Q5
3 N-KB3	P-Q3	9 Q-N3	Q-K2
4 N-B3	N-KB3	10 PxP	PxP
5 B-B4	N-B3	11 K-Q1	P-B3
6 P-Q3	B-KN5	12 P-QR4	KR-N1

Too slow. 12 ... O-O-O (see page 47) is best.

13 R-B1	P-KR3	16 P-B3	B-N3
14 N-K2	O-O-O	17 P-R5	B-B2
15 NxN	BxN	18 B-K3	K-N1

Threatening ... NxP.

19 K-B2	K-R1	20 R-B3	N-Q4?!

This allows 21 PxN, PxP; 22 B-R2, P-K5; 23 B-KB4, PxR; 24 BxB, etc. But Rubinstein prefers to go his own way.

21 B-N1	N-B5	23 P-KN3!	NxRP
22 Q-B2	B-N1	24 RxP!	Q-Q3
		25 Q-N6!!	....

If 25 ... PxQ; 26 PxP dis ch, B-R2; 27 RxBch, K-N1; 28 R/B7xPch, K-B1; 29 B-R6, and Black can resign.

25	....	R-Q2		27	BxQ	R-B7ch
26	B-B5!	RxR		28	QxR!	NxQ
				29	B-B5!	Resigns

Black must lose a piece. White's Bishops are all-powerful.

Game 8: FALKBEER COUNTER GAMBIT
(Hilversum, 1947)

V. CASTALDI		P. TRIFUNOVICH	
White		Black	
1 P-K4	P-K4	3 KPxP	P-K5
2 P-KB4	P-Q4	4 P-Q3	N-KB3
		5 N-Q2	....

This move, strongly recommended in recent years, is by no means so formidable as its reputation.

5	PxP	9 QxQch	KxQ
6 BxP	NxP	10 B-R4	B-KB4
7 N-K4?	N-N5!	11 N-N5	K-K1
8 B-N5ch	P-B3!	12 K-Q1	P-B3
		13 N/5-B3	N/1-R3!

With the troublesome threat of ... N-B4. If White expected relief from the exchange of Queens, he is soon undeceived.

14 P-QR3	R-Q1ch	*19* P-N3	K-B2
15 B-Q2	N-Q4	*20* R-QB1	B-B2
16 K-K2	N-B4	*21* K-B2	B-N3ch
17 B-N3	NxB	*22* K-N2	KR-K1
18 PxN	B-Q3	*23* P-R3	N-K6ch

Black has increased the pressure relentlessly to drive White into a hopeless situation.

24 K-R2	R-Q6	*27* P-N4	B-K5
25 P-QN4	KR-Q1	*28* N-K1	R-Q7ch!
26 B-B3	N-Q8	Resigns	

For if 29 BxR, RxBch; 30 K-N3, B-B7ch; 31 K-R2, BxN/K8ch; with devastating effect. A masterpiece of logical play.

Game 9: PETROFF'S DEFENSE
(British Championship, 1938)

	C. H. ALEXANDER *White*			H. V. MALLISON *Black*
1	P-K4	P-K4	9	PxP	P-KB4
2	N-KB3	N-KB3	10	P-KR3	B-R4
3	NxP	P-Q3	11	N-B3	N-Q2?!
4	N-KB3	NxP	12	NxN	PxN
5	P-Q4	P-Q4	13	BxP	N-B3
6	B-Q3	B-Q3	14	B-B5!	K-R1
7	O-O	B-KN5	15	P-KN4!	NxQP
8	P-B4	O-O?!	16	B-K6!	....

This is the game that discredited Marshall's dashing counter-attack. (Thus far the variation has been given on page 58.) As two of Black's pieces are attacked, his next move is forced.

16	....	B-B2	17	N-N5!

Again Black has no choice, for if 17 ... B-N1; 18 BxB, RxB??; 19 N-B7 mate!—or 18 ... KxB; 19 N-K6, winning as in the text continuation.

17	....	BxB	18	NxB	Q-R5

An ingenious resource: after 19 NxR, QxRP; Black can force a draw. But now comes the real point of the variation—

by guarding his King Rook Pawn, White threatens B-N5, winning the Queen. This gives White time to win the exchange.

| 19 Q-N3!! | N-B5 | 21 NxR | RxN |
| 20 BxN | BxB | 22 K-N2 | B-Q3 |

With the exchange to the good, White has an easy win.

23 Q-K6!	Q-N4	31 R-Q7	P-N4
24 P-B4!	BxP	32 P-Q5	P-QR4
25 QR-K1	Q-QR4	33 R-K7	P-R5
26 Q-K5!	QxQ	34 P-R3	B-Q3
27 RxQ	K-N1	35 RxRch	KxR
28 R-K7	P-KN4	36 R-K6	K-N2
29 P-KR4	PxP	37 KxP	B-B5
30 K-R3	P-KR3	38 K-R5	B-B8
		39 R-K2	Resigns

Black has had enough. A game of outstanding theoretical importance.

Game 10: PETROFF'S DEFENSE
(U.S. Championship, 1940)

I. KASHDAN		A. KUPCHIK	
White		*Black*	
1 P-K4	P-K4	4 N-KB3	NxP
2 N-KB3	N-KB3	5 P-Q4	P-Q4
3 NxP	P-Q3	6 B-Q3	B-K2
		7 O-O	O-O

Inexact. The right way is 7 ... N-QB3; and if 8 P-B4, N-QN5; as shown on page 57.

| 8 P-B4 | N-KB3 | 9 N-B3 | N-B3? |

Another inexactitude, this time a very serious one that gives White a strangle hold on Black's position. Relatively better was 9 ... PxP; 10 BxP, QN-Q2; followed by ... N-N3-Q4.

10 P-B5!	B-N5
11 B-K3	Q-B1
12 R-K1	R-K1
13 P-KR3!	B-K3

14 P-R3	N-N1
15 Q-B2	P-B3
16 N-KN5	P-KN3
17 NxB	QxN
18 B-KN5	Q-Q2

This blocks the development of his Queen Knight—but if 18 ... Q-B1?; 19 RxB, RxR; 20 BxN, etc. The ultimate goal of White's stifling pressure is to gain undisputed mastery of the open King file.

19 R-K3	B-Q1
20 Q-K2	RxR
21 QxR	N-R4

22 R-K1	BxB
23 QxB	N-N2
24 R-K7	Q-Q1

White has the open file, and the seventh rank as well. Material gain is the next step, with an easily won ending.

25 Q-B6	Q-KB1
26 RxNP	N-K3
27 P-QN4	Q-N2
28 QxQch	KxQ
29 N-K2	P-QR4
30 P-N5	PxP

31 BxQNP	N-R3
32 BxN	RxB
33 R-Q7	R-R1
34 RxP	R-QN1
35 P-B6	R-N7
36 R-K5	N-B2
37 N-B3	Resigns

Black's faulty ninth move cost him the game.

Game 11: PHILIDOR'S DEFENSE
(Monte Carlo, 1903)

	C. SCHLECHTER *White*			J. MASON *Black*
1	P-K4	P-K4	5	N-QB3	B-Q2
2	N-KB3	P-Q3	6	B-K2	N-B3
3	P-Q4	PxP	7	O-O	B-K2
4	NxP	N-KB3	8	P-B4	. . . .

Black has chosen the easiest, but not the best, way out. The surrender of the center at his third move leaves his opponent with a lasting plus in mobility.

8	. . . .	NxN	11	B-N2	N-K1
9	QxN	B-B3	12	P-N5	B-Q2
10	P-QN4!	O-O	13	N-Q5	P-KB4

Striving for freedom, he only succeeds in opening the King file for White's use.

14	B-Q3!	P-B3	16	NxBch	QxN
15	NPxP	NPxP	17	QR-K1!	PxP
			18	RxP	Q-B3

Now White simplifies into a won ending.

19 Q-B4ch!	Q-B2	25 RxQP	QRxKBP
20 R-K7!	QxQ	26 RxR	RxR
21 BxQch	P-Q4	27 R-Q8	K-B1
22 BxPch	PxB	28 B-R3ch	K-B2
23 RxB	R-B1	29 R-Q7ch	K-N3
24 R-B2	R-B5	30 RxP	R-B5

Black must regain one of the lost Pawns; but meanwhile White sets up a foolproof winning process.

31 R-K7!	N-B3	33 B-N2	RxP
32 R-K2	R-QR5	34 BxN	KxB

Now White's plan is clear: Black's King cannot block the passed Queen Bishop Pawn.

35 K-B2	P-R4	41 K-N4	R-N1ch
36 K-K1!	P-N4	42 K-R5	R-QB1
37 K-Q2	K-B4	43 K-N5	R-N1ch
38 K-Q3	R-R1	44 K-R6	R-QB1
39 P-B4	R-Q1ch	45 R-B2!	K-K4
40 K-B3	R-QB1	46 K-N7	R-B4
		47 K-N6	Resigns

From this logical game it is all too clear that after Black surrenders the center, his prospects are bleak indeed.

Game 12: PHILIDOR'S DEFENSE
(Stockholm, 1912)

A. ALEKHINE		G. MARCO	
White		*Black*	
1 P-K4	P-K4	4 N-B3	QN-Q2
2 N-KB3	P-Q3	5 B-QB4	B-K2
3 P-Q4	N-KB3	6 O-O	O-O

After this colorless move, Black is limited to an unpromising defensive situation. As indicated on page 70, his best course is to try for ... P-KR3 and ... P-KN4—with possibilities of counterplay.

7 Q-K2	P-B3
8 P-QR4!	P-KR3
9 B-N3	Q-B2
10 P-KR3	K-R2
11 B-K3	P-KN3

12 QR-Q1	K-N2
13 N-KR2!	N-KN1
14 P-B4	P-B3
15 Q-N4!	PxQP
16 BxP	N-B4
17 P-B5!	....

White's position becomes more menacing from one move to the next. If now 17 ... P-KN4; 18 BxN, followed by 19 Q-R5, penetrates Black's defenses.

17	NxB
18 QxPch	K-R1
19 PxN	B-Q2
20 Q-N3	R-B2
21 N-N4	Q-Q1

22 N-K2!	R-N2
23 N-B4	Q-K1
24 Q-R4	Q-B2
25 R-Q3	K-R2
26 N-N6	....

With the nasty threat of 27 R-B4 followed by 28 NxRP!, NxN; 29 QxNch!!, KxQ; 30 R-R4ch and mate next move!

26	RxN
27 PxRch	QxP
28 BxBP	BxN

29 BxB	R-K1
30 RxP	Q-N2
31 B-B6	NxB
32 KRxN	Resigns

Black never really had a chance after his faulty opening play.

Game 13: CARO-KANN DEFENSE
(Vienna, 1928)

H. KMOCH		B. HOENLINGER	
White		*Black*	
1 P-K4	P-QB3	5 N-N3	B-N3
2 P-Q4	P-Q4	6 P-KR4	P-KR3
3 N-QB3	PxP	7 N-B3	N-Q2
4 NxP	B-B4	8 B-Q3	BxB
		9 QxB	KN-B3

Even after the more exact 9 ... Q-B2; *10* B-Q2, KN-B3; *11* O-O-O, P-K3; *12* K-N1, O-O-O; *13* P-B4, Black has a lifeless game. See also page 82.

10 B-Q2	P-K3	11 O-O-O	B-Q3
		12 KR-K1	BxN

Leads to trouble. He should have tried *12* ... Q-B2; *13* N-B5, O-O-O.

13 PxB	Q-N3	14 N-K5	NxN

Or *14* ... O-O; *15* NxN, NxN; *16* P-KN4, with a strong attack.

15 PxN	N-N5	17 B-N5	Q-R4
16 Q-KB3	P-KR4	18 K-N1	NxP

Or *18* ... O-O; *19* B-K7, KR-K1; *20* B-Q6, with winning positional advantage.

19 Q-B4	P-B3

20 BxP!	PxB	22 RxPch	K-B1
21 QxP	N-B2	23 R-Q7	R-R2
		24 RxNch!	Resigns

An unrewarding variation for Black; without offering more than arduous equality, it exposes him to a number of tactical dangers.

Game 14: CARO-KANN DEFENSE
(London, 1947)

R. J. BROADBENT		S. FAZEKAS	
White		*Black*	
1 P-K4	P-QB3	6 N-B3	B-N5
2 P-Q4	P-Q4	7 B-K2	B-Q3
3 N-QB3	PxP	8 O-O	O-O
4 NxP	N-B3	9 P-B4	R-K1
5 NxNch	KPxN	10 R-K1	N-Q2

In the Chess Movie on page 84, Black played 5 ... NPxN and ran into difficulties. The recapture with the King Pawn gives Black a reasonable development, but the resulting Pawn position is against him. For White has four Pawns to three on the Queen-side, and, as we shall see, he knows how to exploit his advantage.

11	B-Q2	QR-B1		16	NxB	RPxN
12	P-KR3	B-R4		17	B-B3	P-KB4
13	B-B3	B-N1		18	Q-Q3	Q-Q3
14	N-R4	Q-B2		19	QR-Q1	P-R3
15	P-KN3	B-N3		20	P-QN4!	....

The Queen-side Pawns are on the way to becoming menacing.

20	....	P-B5		24	PxP	RxR
21	P-N4	Q-B3		25	RxR	NxP
22	K-N2	Q-R5		26	Q-Q4	Q-R3
23	P-Q5!	P-QB4		27	P-Q6	N-K3

White has acquired his passed Pawn—and a very menacing one too. He can now play 28 Q-Q5 with decisive effect, but the continuation he actually selects is also strong.

28	RxN!?	PxR		33	B-R5	R-QN1
29	P-Q7	R-Q1		34	P-Q8/Q	RxQ
30	Q-N6	Q-N4		35	BxR	QxB
31	QxPch	K-R2		36	BxP	P-R4
32	Q-B7!	B-K4		37	B-Q5!	K-R3

White attacks on two fronts. Black must succumb.

38	P-B5!	K-N4	43 Q-N8	P-N4
39	B-B3	Q-Q6	44 B-K4	P-B6ch
40	P-B6	Q-Q3	45 K-R3	PxP
41	P-B7!	QxP	46 Q-R7ch	K-N4
42	P-R4ch!	K-R3	47 Q-N6ch	Resigns

It is mate next move.

Game 15: NIMZO-INDIAN DEFENSE
(Berne, 1932)

A. STAEHELIN
White

A. ALEKHINE
Black

1	P-Q4	N-KB3	4 Q-B2	P-Q4
2	P-QB4	P-K3	5 PxP	QxP
3	N-QB3	B-N5	6 N-B3	P-B4
			7 P-QR3	....

White branches off from 7 B-Q2, as played on page 92.

7	....	BxNch	10 B-K2	P-QN3
8	PxB	N-B3	11 O-O	PxP!
9	P-K3	O-O	12 KPxP?	....

White discards *12* BPxP because it gives Black the Queen-side majority of Pawns. The text is worse, however, as it leaves White with a weak Pawn on the Queen Bishop file.

12	B-N2	17 N-K1	P-QN4
13 R-Q1	QR-B1!	18 Q-N3	Q-KB4
14 P-B4	N-QR4!	19 B-Q3	B-K5
15 Q-R4	NxP	20 BxB?	NxB
16 R-N1	P-QR3	21 P-B3	N-B6!
		Resigns	

White loses the exchange without compensation.

Game 16: NIMZO-INDIAN DEFENSE
(Margate, 1938)

J. R. CAPABLANCA		M. NAJDORF	
White		*Black*	
1 P-Q4	N-KB3	8 BxB	N-B3
2 P-QB4	P-K3	9 R-Q1	O-O
3 N-QB3	B-N5	10 P-QR3	PxP
4 Q-B2	P-Q4	11 NxP	NxN
5 PxP	QxP	12 RxN	Q-B3
6 N-B3	P-B4	13 P-K4	P-K4
7 B-Q2	BxN	14 R-B4	....

This is the position reached at the end of the model variation on page 94. Black is desperately in need of counterplay.

14	Q-K3	16 R-Q5	Q-KN3
15 R-B5	N-Q2	17 P-B3	N-N3!

Black alertly surrenders a Pawn in the hope of stamping the position of White's Queen Rook as unfavorable. This speculation turns out well.

18 RxP	B-K3	21 R-QN5	P-QN3
19 P-B4	Q-R3	22 B-K2	N-B4
20 P-KN3	N-Q2	23 P-QN4	P-R3!
		24 RxP	B-N6!

A very complicated position. If *25 Q-N2, QxR; 26 PxN,
Q-QB3; 27 QxB, QxKP; 28 R-B1, KR-K1; 29 Q-Q1, QR-Q1;
30 B-Q2, R-K2;* and White cannot meet the threat of . . . .
R/K2-Q2 or . . . R/Q1-K1.

25 RxQ	BxQ	28 O-O	N-Q7
26 R-R5	NxP	29 R-B2	KR-B1
27 B-R1	P-B4!	30 B-Q4	P-N3
		31 R-R4	N-K5

Threatening to tie up the unfortunate Rook for good with
. . . P-KR4. White therefore decides to give up the exchange.

32 P-N4	NxR	34 B-B5	RPxP
33 KxN	P-QR4!	35 RPxP	B-N6

After *35 . . . B-K5*; Black retains his winning chances.

36 PxP	R-R7	39 R-K3	K-B2
37 PxP!	PxP	40 K-B3	BxBch
38 R-R3	B-B5	41 RxB	RxR
		42 KxR	. . . .

The ending is a draw.

42	K-K3	44 K-K3!	R-KR1
43 K-B3	K-B4	45 K-Q4!	RxP
		46 K-Q5	Drawn

White's Knight Pawn will cost Black his Rook. A difficult,
exciting game.

Game 17: GRUENFELD DEFENSE
(U.S. Championship, 1938)

S. RESHEVSKY		A. E. SANTASIERE	
White		*Black*	
1 P-Q4	N-KB3	7 KBxP	QN-Q2
2 P-QB4	P-KN3	8 N-B3	N-N3
3 N-QB3	P-Q4	9 B-K2	B-K3
4 B-B4	B-N2	10 Q-B2	KN-Q4
5 P-K3	O-O	11 B-K5	R-B1
6 Q-N3	PxP	12 NxN	QxN
		13 BxB	KxB?

As shown on page 103, the correct move is *13* ... Q-R4ch.
The careless text move allows White to get a strong bind on
the position.

14 P-QN4!	B-B4	22 R-B5	P-K3
15 Q-N2	N-B5	23 QR-QB1	P-QR3
16 Q-N3	N-N3	24 P-QR4	Q-N1
17 Q-B3	Q-Q3	25 P-R3!	BxN
18 P-QR3	N-Q4	26 BxB	KR-Q1
19 Q-N2	B-N5	27 Q-N3	P-B4
20 O-O	P-QB3	28 P-N3	K-B3
21 KR-B1	P-B3	29 K-N2	P-R3
		30 P-R4	P-KN4?

Being at a loss for good moves in his cramped position,
Black resorts to bad ones. It does not take White long to engi-
neer a brilliant breakthrough.

31 P-K4!	BPxP	34 R-K1	K-Q3
32 PxPch	PxP	35 BxN!	KPxB
33 BxP	K-K2	36 R-K5!	R-N1

White is now ready to smash Black's weakened position.

37	R/B5xQPch!	PxR	39	Q-B5ch!	K-Q2
38	QxPch	K-B2	40	Q-K7ch	K-B3
			41	Q-K6ch	Resigns

Game 18: GRUENFELD DEFENSE
(Match, 1950)

	KRYLOV *White*			KOZMA *Black*

1	P-Q4	N-KB3	5	P-K4	NxN
2	P-QB4	P-KN3	6	PxN	P-QB4
3	N-QB3	P-Q4	7	B-QB4	B-N2
4	PxP	NxP	8	N-K2	O-O
			9	O-O	PxP

The main line on page 106 gives 9 ... N-Q2 here.

10	PxP	N-B3	11	B-K3	B-N5
			12	P-B3	N-R4!?

Inviting the Pawn grab 13 BxPch, RxB; 14 PxB, RxRch; 15 KxR, which leaves Black with the initiative.

13	B-Q3	B-K3	15	QxB	P-B3
14	P-Q5!	BxR	16	N-Q4!!	....

The sacrifice of the exchange, characteristic of this variation, gives White a mighty initiative.

16	B-Q2	*19* P-B5!	KPxBP
17 B-KR6	R-K1	*20* PxP	P-KN4
18 P-B4	P-K3	*21* N-K6!	Q-K2
		22 BxP!	....

The main point of White's second sacrifice is that if 22 ... PxB; 23 P-B6, Q-B2; *24* NxP, QxQP; *25* P-B7ch, K-B1; *26* NxPch, K-K2; *27* Q-B6 mate.

22	BxN	*26* BxPch!	KxB
23 BxP	Q-B4ch	*27* R-B7ch	K-R3
24 B-Q4	QxP	*28* B-K3ch!	RxB
25 PxB	RxP	*29* Q-B6ch	Resigns

There is a mate in two. This theoretically valuable game shows how important Black's King Bishop is for the defense, and how sadly it can be missed after the acceptance of the exchange sacrifice.

Game 19: BUDAPEST DEFENSE
(Match, 1946)

C. KOTTNAUER
White

G. MARTIN
Black

1	P-Q4	N-KB3	8	B-Q3	NxP
2	P-QB4	P-K4	9	BxB	NxR
3	PxP	N-K5	10	N-B3	B-B4
4	Q-B2	P-Q4	11	N-K4	Q-K2
5	PxP e.p.	B-B4	12	B-N5	P-KB3
6	N-QB3!	NxQP	13	O-O-O!	N-R3
7	P-K4	NxKP	14	R-Q7	....

Thus far we have the variation given on page 116.

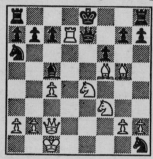

Black must now give up the Queen, for if *14* ... Q-B1; *15* Q-R4!, P-B3; *16* RxQNP is deadly.

14	....	QxR	22	K-Q2	KR-K1
15	BxQch	KxB	23	QxPch	K-Q1
16	NxBch	NxN	24	Q-N8ch	K-K2
17	Q-B5ch	N-K3	25	QxPch	K-B1
18	N-Q4	QR-K1	26	N-Q3!	R/K8-K5
19	Q-Q5ch	K-B1	27	P-B5	N-B7
20	NxN	PxB	28	NxN	R-K7ch
21	N-B5!	R-K8ch	29	K-B3	RxN
			30	P-QN4	Resigns

He is helpless against the Queen-side Pawns.

Game 20: BUDAPEST DEFENSE
(Berlin, 1918)

	A. RUBINSTEIN			M. VIDMAR	
	White			*Black*	
1	P-Q4	N-KB3	*7*	Q-Q5	BxNch
2	P-QB4	P-K4	*8*	PxB	Q-R6
3	PxP	N-N5	*9*	R-B1	P-B3
4	B-B4	N-QB3	*10*	PxP	NxP/3
5	N-KB3	B-N5ch	*11*	Q-Q2	P-Q3
6	N-B3	Q-K2	*12*	N-Q4	O-O
			13	P-K3??	....

Here *13* P-B3 is the recommended move. (See page 120.)

13	....	NxN	*15*	Q-B2	Q-R4ch
14	BPxN	N-K5	*16*	K-K2	....

Now Black is ready for a promising sacrifice of the exchange, which yields him a powerful attack.

16	....	RxB	*21*	K-R4	R-K3
17	PxR	B-B4	*22*	B-K2	R-R3ch
18	Q-N2	R-K1	*23*	B-R5	RxBch
19	K-B3	N-Q7ch	*24*	KxR	B-N3ch
20	K-N3	N-K5ch	*25*	K-N4	Q-R4 mate

Game 21: DUTCH DEFENSE
(Warsaw, 1935)

B. REILLY
White

R. FINE
Black

1	P-Q4	P-K3	4 B-N2	B-K2
2	N-KB3	P-KB4	5 P-B4	P-Q3
3	P-KN3	N-KB3	6 N-B3	O-O
			7 O-O	Q-K1

Thus far the game has followed the variation on page 130. The key to White's strategy is an early P-K4.

8 Q-B2	QN-Q2	13 P-Q5!	P-B4
9 P-K4	N-R4?	14 B-Q2	N-N5
10 PxP	PxP	15 N-N5	Q-Q1
11 R-K1!	QN-B3	16 N-K6	BxN
12 N-KN5!	P-B3	17 RxB	....

White's control of the King file and the K6 square gives him an overwhelming positional advantage.

17	P-QR3	20 N-Q1	P-B5
18 QR-K1!	R-B2	21 B-K4!	P-KN3
19 N-B3	N-K4	22 B-QB3	N-N2

Winning the exchange, but White will have ample compensation.

23	BxN!	PxB	27	PxN	Q-K1
24	N-B3!	R-KB1	28	R-Q7	B-B3
25	R-Q1!	PxP	29	B-Q5!	K-R1
26	RPxP	NxR	30	N-K4	B-N2
			31	N-Q6	....

White simply piles on the pressure.

31	....	Q-N1	36	N-Q6ch	K-R1
32	P-K7!	R-K1	37	Q-K4!	B-Q5
33	N-B7ch!	K-N1	38	K-N2	B-B3
34	NxPch	K-R1	39	Q-K6	BxKP
35	N-B7ch	K-N1	40	Q-K5ch	Resigns

A masterpiece of positional play by White.

Game 22: DUTCH DEFENSE
(Venice, 1948)

M. NAJDORF			H. GROB	
White			*Black*	

1	P-Q4	P-K3	6	QxB	O-O
2	P-QB4	P-KB4	7	N-QB3	P-Q4
3	P-KN3	N-KB3	8	N-B3	P-B3
4	B-N2	B-N5ch	9	O-O	QN-Q2
5	B-Q2	BxBch	10	P-K3	PxP?

This foolish capture puts an end to Black's "stonewall" setup. The following play shows in a most instructive manner how Black is harmed by giving up his solid Pawn formation.

11	Q-K2	P-QN4	14	N-R3!	N-Q4
12	N-N5	N-N1	15	P-K4!	NxN
13	P-KR4!	P-KR3	16	PxN	P-QR4

In return for the sacrificed Pawn, White has an enormous lead in development, which is bound to have a decisive effect.

17 N-B4	K-R2	*20* PxP!	PxP
18 KR-K1	R-R2	*21* P-Q5!	R-Q1
19 P-R5!	Q-B2	*22* QR-Q1	P-B4

23 P-Q6!	RxP	*24* B-Q5!	....

Threatening a mating attack with 25 Q-K8 or even 25 B-N8ch!

24	Q-Q1	*25* Q-K8	....

This leaves Black without a satisfactory reply.

25	B-K3	*26* RxB	Resigns

Black was fittingly punished for giving up his stonewall Pawn pattern.

For free descriptive catalog of all Cornerstone
Library Publications write to:

CORNERSTONE LIBRARY, Inc.
— Dept. 24 —
630 Fifth Ave.
New York 20, N. Y.